SELF ESTEEM

Effective Ways on How to Raise Your Self-esteem

(Find Inner Peace to Develop Willpower With
Guided Meditations)

I0135014

Deanna Hou

Published by Deanna Hooker

Deanna Hooker

All Rights Reserved

Self Esteem: Effective Ways on How to Raise Your Self-esteem (Find Inner Peace to Develop Willpower With Guided Meditations)

ISBN 978-1-77485-381-8

Legal & Disclaimer

The information contained in this book is not designed to replace or take the place of any form of medicine or professional medical advice. The information in this book has been provided for educational and entertainment purposes only.

The information contained in this book has been compiled from sources deemed reliable, and it is accurate to the best of the Author's knowledge; however, the Author cannot guarantee its accuracy and validity and cannot be held liable for any errors or omissions. Changes are periodically made to this book. You must consult your doctor or get professional medical advice before using any of the

TABLE OF CONTENTS

Introduction

Confidence is something everyone should have within them. What we wear, how we act as we walk, talk, and interact with others weighs a lot when it comes to confidence. The confidence we have allows us to be risk-averse and take risks with no fear of what other people might think.

If you are able to complete every task with confidence, you'll greatly enhance the results , and you'll appreciate the process. As you gain confidence your capabilities will increase or appear to. The tasks that seemed so difficult in the past are now so easy to complete in the present, and you'll begin to question why you never made the leap sooner.

Confidence should be regarded as an extraordinary strength since the results you can get from this tiny ingredient is amazing. It is likely that people take the time to take note of your words and your thoughts that were previously, if not expressed, if ever, not even glanced at were now on the forefront and have a lot of value.

Confidence is the state of mind that is not learned or taught. It's the feeling of peace, calm confident, and a belief that you are able to accomplish whatever you put your mind to. You are the sole authority in your own confidence and alone determine the degree to which what other people consider to be their opinions will influence your life in any way.

Many people are not confident because of their low body image and feel uncomfortable about how they appear. It is easy to overcome this by understanding and exploring your body. Be open with yourself regarding your physical appearance and the strengths and flaws associated with it. Find ways to emphasize your best qualities and keep the focus off of the flaws. If you are more at ease in your appearance then you'll start to feel more secure being you, and your confidence will receive the much-needed boost it needs.

Maybe you think you're not educated or well-read enough to express your opinions and suggestions. This can seriously undermine your confidence and level of comfort when you are in a group. Make sure to read the most you can about any topic you are interested in or go to that class you've always wanted but didn't get to. Expand your knowledge and you'll soon feel more comfortable in expressing your thoughts and opinions.

A lot of individuals who made strides in confidence levels abruptly reverse their steps when they fall short in a task. This is not an excuse to be discouraged but instead an opportunity to gain control and demonstrate your determination by persevering until you are successful. This will show your value and you'll be admired by your peers for never giving up on the first sign of an challenge.

There is nothing worth having in life that can be obtained easily and, if you're honest there was no one who ever claimed that it was. Do your best to achieve the things you desire, aim towards your goals with your hand outstretched and a steadfast stride towards the end of the road.

Chapter 1: An introduction to Self-Confidence, Self-Esteem

It is not unusual to hear people refer to self-confidence and self-esteem in the same sentence. Although the two terms are closely linked, they possess distinct definitions. It is possible to experience confidence in oneself without self-esteem and confidence in yourself without self-esteem (though those with confidence in themselves are less confident). This chapter will explain the distinctions between confidence in yourself and self-esteem. The chapter will also discuss the advantages of each and how they impact your daily life.

What is self-esteem?

Self-esteem refers to the feeling of worth and worth you feel about your role on the planet. It's about one's worthiness as a person and their contribution to the world generally. If someone is self-confident it is a general feeling that they live in a good environment. Their perception of the world mirrors the positive feelings they feel towards themselves.

Self-esteem-oriented people generally tend to take good better care of themselves. Of course, the care is subjective. It's not unusual to see people who are overweight and think they don't take good care of themselves. But what happens if the person who is overweight is passionate about cooking or working as an chef? What happens if they gain weight due to seeking to show off their culinary recipes with the world, or because they really love eating? The person is taking charge of themselves through doing something they enjoy.

In contrast, someone with low self-esteem tends to concentrate on acquiring things that will increase their value, popularity and social standing. They may work hard to acquire expensive goods in the expectation that they can make them happier. Self-esteem sufferers often seek ways to relieve the loneliness they feel in their lives and especially when they do not realize their self-esteem issues. They may look for sexual partners or attempt to alleviate the feeling of emptyness by drinking, eating or substances.

The benefits of self-esteem

A healthy self-esteem is crucial for relationships, both with yourself as well as with your surroundings. People who have high self-esteem will be looking for positive experiences and relationships in the world. There are numerous benefits to finding yourself a love for yourself for example:

• A more focused focus on what you can accomplish rather than evaluating your limitations

* More willpower to eat better exercise, take better care of yourself

* Better defense against mental health problems

* More acceptance of you

* A willingness to accept compliments

* Increased capacity to deal with difficult situations

* Avoid negative thoughts about yourself and other people.

* Increased capacity to adjust

Increase confidence in your decisions as well as your ability to make decisions

• The freedom to freely express your thoughts, desires thoughts, feelings, and beliefs

* Improved thinking patterns

Is Self-Confidentiality a thing?

Self-confidence is linked to your actions. In a sense it's responsible for most of the decisions you make in your daily life. Think about how friendly you are. Do you reach out to individuals you admire and invite them to dinner? Do you take action when your boss requests volunteers to help with a client, or do you let others shine? Did you shy away from a job opportunity because you weren't certain you could achieve success? Each of these situations can result from an insecurity about yourself.

Self-confidence, then, is the conviction in yourself that you can accomplish. It's believing that you can accomplish the things you want to achieve and believing that even if you fail, you will know that achieve your goals, you will be ok at the end of the journey. It's simple to boost self-confidence by engaging in your daily life. When you accomplish more and more, you'll increase your confidence. The most important thing is to have faith in yourself to do something new for your first attempt. It is impossible to think you'll be able to accomplish something without first going out of your comfortable zone and attempting it.

Benefits of Self-Confidence

People who feel confident believe they are equipped to be successful in stressful situations. They believe of their ability to achieve. Even if they don't achieve their goals, they believe of their ability to rebound. Here are some looks at ways self-confidence can alter your life:

• Better capacity to influence other people

* More positive attitude

• Greater value and sense of purpose.

A better chance of experiencing new opportunities

* Greater capabilities for leadership

More likelihood of achieving being successful in the world of

* Enhanced attractiveness

Reduced anxiety, particularly when faced with stressful situations.

* Increased motivation and probability of taking actions

There are key differences between Self-Confidence and Self-Esteem

While many think of self-esteem and confidence as closely connected terms however, there are many aspects that differentiate them. When you look at these comparisons, consider which aspects of your own life that you could be having difficulty in. Take note of situations that are like ones you've experienced. You'll be using these as we move on to build self-awareness.

Self-Confidence can be a situational

One of the main distinctions between self-confidence and self-esteem is the way they appear. One who is self-confident generally feels confident regardless of circumstances. If they feel confident about their job They generally feel confident about the job they perform in their home and beyond the workplace. Self-confidence, however is subject to change depending upon the circumstance. A person could be extremely confident about their abilities to manage or work as part of teams, yet lack confidence when it comes to calculating numbers or participating in sports. You can feel confident in one part of your life but be unsure in other. Self-confidence is a domain-specific issue, however self-esteem is a universal concept that can be found in all aspects of our lives.

A clear example of this is the former professional tennis player Andre Agassi, who is widely regarded as one of the top tennis players of the past. It is evident the fact that Agassi is confident about his skills as a player despite claims later that his dislike of tennis was a result of his childhood. While Agassi excelled at tennis however, he struggled with self-confidence and a general lack of self-confidence in other areas that he was involved in. Recently, Agassi has revealed his experience with depression anxiety, depression, and substance abuse and has made it clear that even those who are competent or successful in their chosen track can be afflicted by low self-esteem.

Building Self-Confidence. Building Self-Esteem

It is generally easy to develop confidence in yourself than self-esteem. Self-confidence can be developed through practice or by being proficient at doing something. As people progress across their journeys, they'll have accomplishments and their lists of talents and achievements continue to expand. While these accomplishments can boost self-confidence, they are not enough to increase self-esteem. Self-esteem can't be improved by creating an arsenal of abilities when those skills don't improve a person's opinion of them.

Factors that affect self-esteem

Self-esteem grows as time passes. When you're young self-esteem means that you are content externally. Friends at school and siblings, parents and any other family members you are close to play an important influence on how you feel about yourself. If they provide positive feedback, it can help increase confidence in yourself. In the same way, how they treat you can affect the way you view your contribution to the world.

One reason why individuals struggle with self-esteem is the fact that they weren't given the positive encouragement and the confidence they required to recognize that they are worthy within the society. People with low self-esteem remain in a state of struggle when they become teenagers. Even if they get praise from peers, they could still be unable to handle the judgement or criticism of their parents. There are a variety of things that impact self-esteem when you're an adult. This includes:

The perception you have of other people

What others think of you

* How you see other people

Experience in the workplace or at school

* The presence of illness or disability

* Traditions of religion or culture

In these various aspects those that you control the most in are thoughts and standing. It's likely that many of the strategies offered for improving your self-esteem are focused on changing your thinking and how you view things around you. This allows for change to occur from within.

Factors that Influence Self-Confidence

Self-confidence grows as time passes. When you acquire new abilities, you get more confident about these skills. Although skills can boost confidence in yourself, they are not the only factor in playing. These are some other aspects that impact confidence:

* Possessing a positive self-image

* Your view of the world

* Ability to manage the criticism and errors

• How others who are around you regard you

Self-esteem and confidence are two distinct traits Certain strategies can be employed to boost the growth of both. However, there are other methods that could be more effective in improving either one and the other. It is highly recommended to go through all chapters, since each chapter helps you develop the foundation of your personal development. It will help you increase your confidence, take advantage of new opportunities, experiment with different things, and possess the self-love that allows you to build positive relationships as well as make sensible decisions regarding your life.

Chapter 2: What is A Healthy Mindset? And What Is It To Have One?

Before we get into the intricacies of a healthy mind and the best way to create and sustain it we must first define the word'mind'. It's an abstract concept used to define thoughts, emotions self-awareness, and subjective states we believe to originate out of our minds.

The Mind:

The term has been the subject of fascination for a long time. Rene Descartes, a philosopher who came up with the concept of dualism. It is a reference to the relation between our mind as well as body. This idea was the subject of debate for philosophers, psychologists, and physiologists as it was developed.

The thoughts that our minds produce are extremely abstract. Many attempts were made to discover these abstract ideas such as beliefs, feelings, and thoughts and how they are created by the brain. Today, a majority of people are able to agree that the mind was created through the brain. A few religions believe that the origin for the brain is supremacy of the soul. Several were in a debate that the brain is the only thing that can be responsible for all of the mind's actions.

* Things you didn't realize in your head:

Your mind is among the most mysterious and elusive things. Here are a few things you may not know concerning your thoughts.

You don't know your mind:

As I stated in the past, no one knows what the mind actually is and where it came from. The brain that gives birth to the mind. It is an opinion of the majority. I'm saying that because sometimes your mind operates without relying on your brain. This is a little odd. The mind is something we are aware exists, but we don't know its origins.

Thinking is similar to speaking to yourself:

The thoughts that pop into your head are thoughts that you tell yourself. It's like talking to yourself, much like self-talk. When you are looking to find out what's on your mind then you tell yourself what conversation you're engaging in with yourself.

*You will be able to see your mind's workings:

It is possible to master mind-watching , without interfering in your skull or your brain or skull in any manner. By being aware that you are, you can sit back and observe your mind do things as if you were observing the events of an individual rather than experiencing it by yourself. Being aware of your mind, or, in other words the observer self is in some way detached from emotions and is able to see your thoughts and actions without bias. On the other hand this part of the brain that is able to perceive things has sensory impressions and is connected to emotional responses.

This is vital because when you observe your habits and thoughts like ideas of stories, fantasies and stories You are then able to make changes to your thinking. When you're observant that you can easily keep track of your actions. You should develop their observing self.

How? Be aware of what your brain says or what it says and not be judgmental. Do you find the same thoughts keep your mind occupied and cause you to worry over it again and over again? What are the best ways to talk to yourself? constructive or negative?

Be attentive to your self-talk and you'll be able to see your mind get into action. Then you are able to alter your thinking habits at any time in your life to the way you'd like to.

Your mind is wild and must be controlled:

An Buddhist writer describes wildness of the mind asfollows "(Sometime) you'll encounter the sudden realization that you're completely insane. It is your mind that is screaming crazy, giggling madhouse that are chugging along pell-mell down the hill, totally in control and lost. There's no issue. You're not any more insane than the day before. It's always been this way , and you have never noticed."

It is true that the mind is full of its own tales of fantasies, dreams, and wild imaginations which are always happening. It is not an easy job, however, one can certainly learn to control it. If you find your mind's thoughts telling you bizarre fantasies and stories You tell yourself that these are just thoughts that shouldn't be considered serious. This is a technique of Zen meditation however, one does not have to be a meditation practitioner to enjoy engaging in it.

*Your mind can alter the way you think. brain's functions:

Your thoughts, or should be I say your thoughts can change your brain. It may sound strange however, when you begin to develop new patterns of thought your brain begins to alter its wiring. If you begin to practice something new and you begin to practice it, the same neurons in the brain start functioning and wiring together. This means that changing your mindset changes the way your brain functions.

If you'd like to alter how your brain functions and how you think modify the conversation you engage in with yourself. If, for instance, you're anger and frustrated with your own mistakes or mistakes, try telling you that making mistakes is part of growing and learning. Then, you can try to do better every time.

This way your pattern of thinking will change.

Simple words can bring your mind to tranquility:

Any emotion you feel at any given moment Give it a name or identify it. Studies have shown that labelling your emotions and feelings can reduce and alter the emotions that are causing you stress and make you more at ease with yourself. The act of labeling your emotions can shift your brain's activity into the thought part of the fight or flight area. It's incredible to realize that even a single word can cause damage the brain.

Your mind can aid your brain create a positive mood:

Our brains have a negative bias. This means it is prone to create strong reactions to negative things like dangers, dangers, dangers and errors, as opposed to positive things like a positive experience, joy, and happiness. Although this characteristic that the brain has assisted us to survive, by alerting us to the dangers and risks that are possible however, it can be difficult to relax, feel content and be content.

Fortunately that our minds can aid our brains feel more content. When our minds are trained to concentrate upon the good things in life, it prompts the brain to structure itself to alter the way we feel about things. Be aware of the positive and enjoyable experiences in your life.

Don't let them fade away and forget them. Remain in the memory for a longer period of time to help your brain become more focused on positive things rather than negative things.

*Brain develops as you master new skills regardless of your age:

The process of absorbing new information helps to improve your brain. The research suggests that learning triggers changes in the memory section that your brain. It affects both young and old ones. Oliver Sacks, a neurologist, says,

"Every when we try to master an previous skill or master new ones, our neural connections get strengthened eventually neurons form more neural connections with other neuron. New nerve cells may be developed."

Learn new things regularly to ensure that your brain is functioning properly.

Do you think it's about being healthy in your body, a positive mindset, or both?

We frequently discuss being healthy. But what does it actually refer to being healthy? How can being healthy impact your body and your soul? The definition of healthy depends on the specific you are discussing in terms of.

One of the aspects is a healthy body . The other is a well-balanced mind. To achieve a healthy body, we consume foods which have positive effects upon our body. We exercise, visit the gym and take part in everything to look physically healthy and keep our body strong. But what about the mind that is healthy?

Are we taking steps to build a healthy mind? What is really needed to be done in order to get one? Like we place healthy substances into our bodies to ensure we are healthy, our minds require positive substances for its health function. In this case, the word "good" refers to healthy substances which have a positive impact on our minds and bodies.

I've seen a lot of people who go to the gym or going for walks, and making meetings with nutritionists, making decisions about what to eat and not consume. That's good. Everyone should do it. But, do they all doing their mind work with the same passion? A healthy mind and body are inextricably linked. Healthy bodies help build a positive mental state and vice to. There's plenty to do for to have a positive mind other than exercises and eating healthy foods.

Why are we talking about having a positive and healthy mental attitude? Why is there such a lot of effort required to set your mind on the right way? This is due to the fact that our brain continues to accumulate thoughts that somehow relate to different experiences in life. The actions we take are also influenced by the thoughts we have. When someone takes charge of his physical health, he will be careful about the unhealthy food items because it is a conscious fact that sugar and junk foods can adversely affect your health. It doesn't regardless of how much physical activity is done, the excessive consumption of these items will cause an effect of its own.

In the same way, when we speak of maintaining an enlightened mindset, this means that we must be aware of the thoughts and beliefs that can negatively impact it. If you are able to maintain an optimistic mindset it helps you to become more loving and accepting. You are attentive, aware of the world around you and are inquisitive.

Although a healthy body and healthy minds are interconnected but they're not the same.

The reason for this lies in the fact that, even though are a fit body, but have a sluggish mind, you are not classified as a healthy person.

There's a quote that I was told that you can eat the most broccoli in the world , but If you don't like your spouse, you'll always be unhealthy. What exactly is that? It means that if you inner self isn't conforming to moral standards, and your mind is simply being negative and absorbing negativity regardless of your physical health you will not be considered to be healthy overall.

You may have seen people in your life who appear physically healthy but do not have anything positive coming out of their mouths. They look pretty from an appearance but when you get to know them or meet them, they'll be the worst people you could never dream of. When I say mental health issues, I don't mean just being morally wrong, but mental disorders such as anxiety, stress depression and so on. can also mean that you're not mentally healthy or, that is you're not feeding your mind the right food.

If you are constantly feeding inappropriate and negative thoughts to your mind, whether regarding yourself or those around yourself, you're more likely to be suffering from mental issues. For example, if think to yourself that, "I am not good enough", "People will never accept me", "The world is cruel", "Nothing will go well to my situation", "Everybody around me is selfish" And other similar things, you are more prone to anxiety, stress, social anxiety depression, and stress. The self-esteem and confidence deteriorates to an extreme degree.

Chapter 3: The Factors that Influence Self-Confidence

There are a myriad of aspects that influence the level of confidence we feel at any given point throughout our life. These elements range from reality of our surroundings to events that have occurred many earlier in our lives. One method to increase confidence in yourself is to be aware of these issues and then address them to overcome them. Some of them you can tackle by yourself, while others require the assistance of a psychoanalyst or psychotherapist. Let's take a look at the most frequent of these issues and offer solutions to these issues.

Unhealthy Parenting

A lot of couples get married due to their love or simply because they like the idea of marriage without taking into consideration all the possibilities that marriage can bring and the obligations that go with it. Being a parent and caring for them is one of the most important elements of marriage that are subject to in the absence of. Many parents believe that parenting is just about having children, providing the money they need and sharing their photos to social platforms. While these are all good things but there are some elements of parenting that when left unchecked, can cause a lot of harm to the lives of kids.

Being present physically and emotionally for your kids is an essential aspect of parenting and shouldn't be left to fend for itself. I understand that the current state of our economy today has forced parents to be extremely active if they want manage to pay for the charge of their families. In the midst of the seemingly unchallenging competitiveness that the majority of people appear to have, an average family might prefer to have the type of life that other families share in social networks. But , it is important to organize your life in a way so that you'll always have time to take care of your children.

There may be nannies in your home who provide care for the children in your home, however there's only what a nanny has the capacity to accomplish. The nanny is not able to substitute for the parent in the child's life, and the child will always be able to tell when parents aren't emotionally present regardless of the amount they offer. Your children should be aware of your presence. There's a sense of assurance that comes from knowing that daddy and mommy are always available and have been there for you.

Children are affected by a variety of things that parents may not be aware of . If you're always absent as parent, your children aren't going to have the sort of emotional connection they need to share their day-to-day struggles.

Consider bullying for instance. Children are often targeted at school and your child could be among those children. Be the type of parent your children feel comfortable to share their struggles with throughout their lives.

There is a particular instance of the bond between fathers and daughters. Studies have shown that daughters whose fathers played an active role in their childhood tend to feel more confident in their lives, much more than it could have been in the absence of fathers. If she is confident that her dad has her back, she is able to set out and conquer the world with a lot of confidence. A girl who is used to hearing "I am in love with the way you look" or "You are beautiful" by her father is not likely to be drawn by those phrases when they are spoken by males in the near future.

Always say positive things to your children. Do not be negative about them. Every word you speak to children can play a role in the development of their brain and their thinking. Be cautious about when you speak to your children.

If you, as an adult have experiences of negative parenting and negative parenting, you don't need to be stuck in the rot due to your parents' choices. You are able to and should elevate yourself above the your past negative experience and be positive from now on. Most important is to understand what the issue really is. If you think your self-confidence lack is due to parental negligence, you can change the story; you can be so confident in yourself that you'll be loved back to positivity.Early trauma

Neglect from parents isn't the only thing that happened to you in your childhood that could cause loss of self-confidence. A more serious issue could be childhood trauma, and the most common of these are rape and sexual assault. If children are raped and sexually assaulted the child typically feels like the incident occurred because they're not worthy and did not deserve the punishment. The rape victims typically feel, and this is often the reason why they are hesitant to speak up regarding the experience. Most rape victims believe that others will judge the victim when they learn about the incident, which is why they don't want to speak to talk about it.

The worst part is that this incident will affect the rest of their lives, if the incident is not addressed. There are a few rape victims who are either extreme in their sexual life or they are afraid of sexual contact and do not desire to engage in any sexual activity with anyone else or sexual relations with everyone who is interested in having sexual relations with them. Whatever the case they lack any self-esteem.

Another cause of early childhood trauma can be watching a family member die. What this can do to the child who is traumatized is that they feel that there is no intrinsic reason to exist and that they are able to live their lives however they wish because they are fated to die. Whatever the cause of the incident the victim should seek out the help from a therapist in order to help them think towards the correct direction. If you're one of those individuals, before doing anything else in your quest of self-confidence, it is essential to figure this out. Seek the help of a therapist and you begin to recognize your worth , and build confidence in yourself. This could be a important step to take as most people are unaware of their circumstance. However, you are aware of what is essential here and you need to take the proper steps.

Social Influence

We looked at the subject in a couple of chapters earlier. society expects you to appear different from what you would like to be. This can be the case in the society we live in . And what is so sad is that people tend to reduce their personality in order to be the persona society expects to see them as. It is impossible to be successful at being somebody else. You are the your best self as you're the one person in the entire world that can do this. If you allow your self to be tossed around by the dictates and whims of society, you'll lose control of your the world and your self-confidence will be blown away.

If you're determined to build self-confidence then you need to be determined to stand up to the norms of society. It's only what you let affect you that will be able to have an impact over your lifestyle. Certain things can affect us in a subliminal way and we may not be aware that they affect us, yet we must be aware. For instance, advertisements and how they're doing to the human mind. Advertising can make you perform actions you don't would like to do. Advertisers use advertisements to make you believe that you need something you know inside that you don't really want or need. If they show your favorite star in front of you holding the item then you begin to think of the product with the celebrity and think that if it's good for the famous and wealthy person, then it should be beneficial for you, too. You'll lose the ability to make your own decision about what you would like to purchase.

The business sector is where we see the greatest instances of societal pressures in the present. Consumers are regarded as the most powerful, yet there's not a single consumer who is making their own choices. It is a phenomenon known as social proof, in which consumers of a product take into consideration the opinions of other customers regarding the product before making a decision on whether to purchase to purchase it on their own.

While this aids in making consumer choices but it also has the potential of causing people to lose confidence in their personal judgement. It is commonplace to claim that you love something but not necessarily because you really love it however, but due to the fact that someone else supported the item. This is what the current increase in social proof has done to our minds.

Cyberbullying is also increasing and is among the main reasons why many people aren't comfortable enough with their authentic selves on social media. But how do you let people who aren't even in contact with you to bully you? Everyone online can be found saying or doing whatever it is they like behind their keyboards and so why do some users allow other people to harass them? The reason is that the people who suffer from bullying online aren't sufficiently confident to speak out on their own behalf. These are typically the same people who participate in boot licking on and offline. They do not make their own decisions and support them. They just wait until their favorite people have spoken. They make their opinions like appendages.

Peer Pressure

In addition, societal influences can be peer pressure. It is known as the reason behind many people who aren't competent enough to take their own decision. The tale that follows of Mark and Cindy in this article will serve as an excellent illustration of this issue:

Mark as well as Cindy had been lovers for a long time. They been dating for five years. They were so in love that they decided to make their love official and wed. Mark was the type of man who could be called the dream of every woman. He loved Cindy with all his heart and was always willing to do anything to make her happy. He did not want to see her in a sad state and would do anything to ensure that there always was smiling on Cindy's faces. Cindy was his top first priority.

Cindy herself was a fan of Mark and admired him and was willing to go the extra mile to make him feel happy. Their union seemed as if it came from heaven, and was highly praised by all and their families, too. offered them a lot of encouragement. Couples even asked what they did to make it happen so flawlessly.

The couple remained happily married until a certain man known as Zed was able to move into the neighborhood. Zed had some issues getting settled and which is why Mark offered him some assistance and he agreed. They began to talk and soon began to become friends. Mark introduces Zed at his wedding to wife Cindy as well as let Cindy know that they'd become acquaintances, something that was not necessary since Cindy knew that Zed spent time with him. Mark rarely made friends and Cindy was happy that he had a friend who whom he actually liked.

Mark and Zed's relationship began to develop, and quickly Zed was expressing opinions on Mark's marriage. Zed told Mark Zed that Mark was not letting Cindy influence him, and which meant that he had given Cindy too much freedom. Mark was unable to understand exactly what Zed was saying initially because he believed that his marriage was going perfectly, which meant that whatever strategy that he and Cindy used was working.

But , you're aware of the fact that is that when pressured by peers it is that you are able to accept it slowly and, before you realize what's going on, you're already acting in line with the direction you've been receiving. That's what happened with Mark. He was soon listening to Zed. He was having more drinks outside with him. He even missed the time he would normally spend with his wife.

Mark wasn't a drinker until meeting Zed however, he slowly deteriorated to the point of being drunk. Mark began looking for excuses to get into fights with Cindy and would always complain about her. Cindy was shocked. Mark was her best friend for a long time and she was not accustomed to this type or treatment from him in any way. The family members complained, but this made it worse for Mark to the point of causing him more pain. He claimed that it was a sign of disdain. He claimed he was a man enough to resolve his own issues--if any. He said he didn't like interference from an outside entity.

Mark did not return to his former self, and Cindy became irritated with the new man. Cindy sought a divorce that Mark took pride in accepting. However, it took just two weeks of being without Cindy before Mark realized what he'd caused himself. He was devastated and set out to find Cindy. He wanted her back , and was eager to pay the price to her and get it the right thing again. However, she was scared of reuniting with him since it took several months to reach the point at which she took the decision to walk away. She was not willing to go through that once more.

Do you know that If Mark believed of himself and the possibility of making the right choices regarding his life and the marriage, he would not have fallen victim to pressure from peers; he would have expressed gratitude to Zed to express his concerns, but insisting that both he and Cindy were in good shape and would prefer to not bother with it. Confident people also face pressure from peers just like any other person, however, their reactions to it are constantly different, and something they'll be proud of in the near future.

Confident Affirmations

I am confident in myself and my abilities to accomplish whatever I want to. I don't care about the things I've gone through. My success is above everything. I am the boss of my life. I trust myself.

Chapter 4: What to do to reduce fears and insecurities through Experiments in the Real World.

Do you feel anxious about being in a group of people? Do you get worried when you're planning meeting new friends?

Understanding the Issue

If that's the case, you must to figure out the reason. Also, you must identify the elements when you are in the crowd or meeting new people which make you feel anxious. There is a pattern to the way anxiety or fear grows. In the majority of cases, it begins with the trigger. The fear could begin when you are told that you must attend the social gatherings. Many introverts are only averse to social events when they do not anticipate it. Some people are afraid when they are required to participate in an activity which draws on them. The fear usually is due to their performance in a social context.

It is perfectly normal to be scared. It's a natural process to alert our body of the danger. However, it could be debilitating socially, especially when fear becomes a way of hindering us from performing our jobs.

Let's take Mike for an example. Mike will soon enjoy his third Christmas with the company. He didn't go to the first two Christmas celebrations of the company as there are always events that make him feel humiliated. He tries to persuade himself into participating in the event, but his fear is always the winner. In the last couple of years, the man usually chooses, at the spur of the moment to stay home and invent an excuse for why he won't attend.

The last two holidays celebrations, Mike did not understand why he didn't wish to go. As he thought about the patterns of his anxiety, he realized it was his behavior in the crowd which made him nervous. He was enthralled by the thought of enjoying a great time with his colleagues and enjoys speaking to a few of them. However, whenever the thought of doing something in front of his colleagues pops into his head and he starts to get anxious. He starts to think of scenarios where it is difficult to perform.

Knowing the specific portion of the party Mike is afraid of, he might be able to stay clear of the part where he performs instead of avoiding the entire party completely.

Triggers are the thoughts about social activities that create anxiety in your brain. The moment the fear is triggered the person who is anxious about social situations is prone to a series of behaviors which will cause them to stay away from certain social occasions. In the workplace the absence of certain events and events could be considered as not being an effective team player.

To avoid your social anxiety from preventing your from doing something you must to determine the exact cause of your anxiety. Here are a few most common social events that people are afraid of:

* Public speaking

Doing something even though an enormous crowd is watching

The feeling of being teased or laughing at

* Presenting before those with authority

* Going out on a date, or having a meeting with someone who you're romantically interested in

* Performing on stage

* Engaging in an informal conversation

Most of the time, people are aware that the things that they worry about the most do not really matter and they are able to overcome it. But, some introverts fail to have the courage to confront their fears even though they are aware that the scenario they are imagining might not take place. Here are a few actions you can take to stop your fear from overtaking your actions:

Control the way you think to deal with your fears

There are certain thought patterns that anxious people commonly utilize. Here are a few of them:

* Assumptions, predictions and assumptions

People who are nervous think that there will always be a chance in their lives to feel embarrassed. They make numerous assumptions that result in their anxiety. They also make predictions about what will happen. For those who suffer from social anxiety the behavior becomes habitual.

If you start thinking and anticipating frightening scenarios It is a sign that you must distract your thoughts from the fear. There are different ways to cope to deal with anxiety. If you're in the workplace when fear strikes it is possible to distract your thoughts with work to keep it from dominating your thoughts.

* Extremely negative thoughts

The beliefs and expectations of introverts suffering from social anxiety tend to be aggravated by their extreme negative attitude. When they think about these situations they think of the most awful things that can occur.

* Personalizing

When they think of issues that could go wrong at social gatherings They also think about how people at the gathering will react to them. They believe that the people in the party want to laugh at them. They think that their bosses are out to humiliate them.

* The fight or flight response

If the fear is triggered the stress hormones trigger their fight or flight response. For introverts with social anxiety the first reaction is to stay clear of the event. They might have made the decision not to go to the event previously and ended up being right. If they ever faced similar stress they chose to employ similar responses to the stress.

In time these habits of mind become automatic when called upon to participate in events they do not know about. The continued use of these patterns of behavior and thinking prevents individuals from enjoying the social benefits.

How do you avoid social Fears?

Exercises to breathe

Breathing is among the very few tasks that the body is able to perform using both the subconscious and conscious mind. Being capable of controlling the unconscious actions of breathing by being aware of them is a potent instrument. One of the initial signs of anxiety is an increase in the rate of breathing in shallow breaths. It can happen in the event that you are about to attend the event. It can also happen when you are thinking about the occasion. If you are experiencing this it is important to regain control over your breathing. For instance, if you sense that you're feeling anxious or nervous about a particular social event then you must sit in your seat and practice the following breathing exercises:

1. Sit down and lie back on the chair , keeping you back upright and head towards the front. Place one hand in your lap and the left hand on your stomach.

2. Take a slow, deep breath through your nose and expand your stomach as air in. You should take at least 4 seconds to breathe in. Keep the air in for two seconds before you take a slow exhale. Breathe through your mouth. It shouldn't take

longer than 4 seconds to breathe all the air.

3. Do this for two to 2 minutes, or till you feel comfortable. When you're done, your fast-paced breathing that is shallow should have stopped.

Change your anxiety-related behavior by taking actions in relation to countering your fears

Most people find that the response to flight develops into a habit following the trigger. At first an introvert who is socially anxious might still attempt to convince himself that he should attend the occasion. In time, the introvert is no longer interested in going. When the idea of going to an event causes him to feel uncomfortable He decides immediately not to attend.

You can alter this habit even if you've been doing it for years. The only thing you need to do is pinpoint the reason behind your anxiety and then explain in detail what behavior results from it. You must then determine the satisfaction you feel when you decide not to go to an event out of anxiety.

After you've recognized the cycle of your routine, you must to connect negative feelings with the practice. Imagine the negative results that the behavior has caused. Create a list to recall the negative impact of the habits had for you. This will convince your mind that this habit isn't helping you in any way.

The next step is to create a new behavior as a result of the trigger. Like we said it is the trigger that triggers first. Then comes the routine of habit. The trigger sensation and anxiety will be present. It's impossible to alter that. But you can alter your behavior in response to the fear. If you're a person who avoids the family dinners during the holidays due to a embarrassing event. Each time you think of the incident, you feel ashamed within. As time passes, this feeling has turned into a fear that the exact incident will occur in the near future.

It is your decision to take the plunge. You should not be arguing with yourself or rethink the option to go or not. Once you've made the decision that you'll be going to the next location and you are ready, the next hurdle will be thoughts that bring back the memories of your embarrassing moment. To ensure that it doesn't affect your decision, seek out a method to modify your behavior each time the memories of your experience occur in your mind.

Instead of worrying about it, simply say "I'm planning to" and then think of a different idea. When your anxiety about social gatherings is a problem, repeat this sentence. By expressing it, you create confidence in the majority of people. It is a sign of change in habits that will lead them back to social gatherings to be successful.

Finally, you must determine the trigger before it occurs. Each time you experience the anxiety, begin to anticipate the behaviour that will follow. Then, you should employ the same phrase as above or any other variation of it in order to keep your mind from getting into habit.

Let your mind be exposed to your fears

One of the most effective strategies to face anxiety is to confront it head on. It is possible to feel overwhelmed should you face all your fears in one go. Better to tackle them in small pieces. Instead of attending every social event you're invited to, concentrate your attention on only one. After you've attended the event, you need to think about the next one that you'll attend. It is important to ensure that the worst-case scenario you imagine in your mind is the result of your fear-based thinking and is likely to never happen.

After attending numerous social events, you'll start to appreciate the event. You'll begin to build confidence in yourself when you're worried regarding an activity. As you attend many events over time, the routine of attending these events begins to form. When that habit is established, this is when magic occurs and your confidence takes an obvious turn to the highest. It's all about changing your routine.

Chapter 5: Goals and Achievements

The steps we've taken in order to increase our self-esteem and personal growth are centered around how we view our bodies. Redefining our views of the self image we have and accepting the things we are able to and cannot change, but most importantly, accepting our identity as we are as individuals. We then took a hard look at the world around us and saw peace and beauty both in the world , and within our heart. It's time to begin to look at our ambitions. We must set out on our own paths and pursue those things we'd like to have. To aim for the stars , but not stop after we've found our way in the midst of them. The most important dreams we cherish and the goals we'd love to accomplish. Our deepest of dreams and most epic fairy stories. It's like all the time that our desires are farther away than ever before. It's as if we'll have to traverse the mountains, canyons or traverse oceans, seas, fields and sands. It's not the situation. No matter what your desires or dreams. No matter how far-fetched your dream or wish. It is possible to achieve it with the effort. It's true that if your desire is to become a famous Hollywood actor, it's likely to take time, but it's not difficult. The idea that it is impossible is the reason it's only it. The act of putting something away from your reach can also reduce your reach. The only person who restricts your own capabilities. The vastness that you see is the you are able to see and the distance you are able to travel. It isn't a problem to travel for long distances if you have to do. If you are locked in a space with a limited number of options the possibilities for you to achieve your goals are a waste of time. If you believe that you're not capable of it and you don't, then you never will. That being said let's get going on making that dream a reality and unlocking the potential to achieve your goals. You can then begin to aim to the sky.

Day Thirteen

What are you hoping to accomplish? What are the things you want to achieve? What were the goals you had as a child or even the ones you are currently living. Whatever you'd like to achieve Don't hesitate to voice it. Perhaps you'd like to write a book or even a collection of books. Perhaps you'd like to race a marathon, or perhaps something smaller, or you'd like to create a recipe that you can perfect within the kitchen. Whatever you want to do you want to achieve, it can be done totally and completely. There's nothing on earth that you aren't able to do but it will require time as well as all the energy you're able to put into it. Do not limit yourself based on the opinions of others about what is feasible, or your own beliefs about what you're capable of, since the chances are you're not. We don't really know what we're skilled until commit ourselves to the challenge of achieving our goals. To be a dreamer to have a mindset that recognizes the potential for being successful. To be successful , you must believe that your dreams are able to be realized. All you need is the determination to go out and pursue them, without taking the word "no" for an answer. Anyone can be the person who is successful, you only need to be motivated and possess the desire to go after it. Today could be the day you begin with, and what else could it be? For day thirteen, we're going to come up with what we would like to achieve. Don't listen to the voices that insist that you shouldn't accomplish anything. The voice within you will critique the things you are looking for. Do not listen, because it's not right, no matter what you think. It isn't sure the extent to which you're capable or, even more importantly, does not want to reveal its secrets. It's trying to hide your talents from you so that you remain on the lowest level of your life. It is hindering your from moving to the upper level to your full potential. If you can think of something, however large or small, you must be able to think about it and note it down. Create something that you are passionate about and something you want. Make a decision to be outrageous and do something you've always thought impossible and the best part about it is that you are able to. It's just a matter of some time and effort however, as I mentioned earlier, the hard work is worth it and you're happy that you gave it best.

Day Fourteen

It's a thrilling experience when you are able to think, when you become overwhelmed by the infinite possibilities that life has to offer. When you let your thoughts wander and you come up with scenarios after scenarios of your own personal accomplishment or grandiosity. It's an exciting process, making up the perfect life or career. What you're looking for is in your mind, ready for the choosing. It's impossible not to be lost in your thoughts and imagine the perfect thing until life becomes dull. It is important to think but not dream with realism So let's be able to step away from the dream for a second. Examine the item you wrote down last night, and then decide on the best way to accomplish it. If the goal will take a lot of time, acknowledge the fact that you need to be realistic and honest with yourself. If you have a goal which is easier to achieve, then be aware of this too. In the end, you must make yourself feel confident that what you wrote down is something you are able to go out and obtain. Don't let yourself be demotivated by the length of time. It's all dependent on the amount of effort you're willing to put in the effort. I know that life can throw some unexpected surprises at times But, remember that excuses can be a deterrent. It's a lot easier to think of obstacles that stop you from reaching your goals, when the truth is that you're scared. It's easy to be afraid, but doing the right thing and achieving your goals is frightening. In my experience, I've had to fall victim to these pitfalls before. Change isn't easy and pursuing your goals requires you to adapt and keep growing like self-esteem is. Take the confidence you have, and tell yourself you're capable of doing it, and keep pushing forward. Day 14 is a day of self-confidence. Say to yourself that you can be confident, and tell yourself that it's acceptable to desire something. Small or large, challenging or simple, it's acceptable. You can get anything you want, since you are worthy of it, and you ought to be able to enjoy it. Make sure you achieve it by encouraging yourself to achieve it. You won't be able to accomplish that without the correct attitude but having confidence will get you to the next level.

Day Fifteen Empowerment is an enormous tool to help you move forward in the right direction, however, on its own it is just a stationary tool, to be successful in your endeavor you require more. Moving forward simply means moving forward and taking steps forward. Re-evaluate your goals and today is the day when we begin to take the first step toward the goal. This is when we can ensure we turn it into a bit less of a fantasy and more of a reality. It's the way of things. that appears unbelievable, we make ourselves believe that it's impossible to achieve or requires an individual who is a certain type of individual. In reality, you're a particular type of individual. The real is more real than we imagine. Before you start the first step, you must understand what you are trying to accomplish. If you need more than one day of action to accomplish and then congratulations for having a big dream and don't let yourself be discouraged. Day 15 is the day to take actions and pursuing your goal. Find out the first thing you have to do in order to turn your dream into become a reality, then go out and achieve it. Perhaps you've had a desire to write a novel So, come up with an idea, purchase an notebook and begin writing. You are an actor? Get started studying, take an class and complete scenes. If it appears that I'm simplifying this, it's not. It's not that difficult when you are determined and never abandon your goals. Whatever you'd like to achieve or accomplish you can achieve it, simply begin. This is the day to do this, so do not let it slip by as you contemplate your choices. Don't let a history of self-esteem issues prevent you from having the life you've always wanted and you are able to achieve everything. When you decide to pursue something that you are passionate about your self-esteem will increase and so will your confidence. This is a growth process on its own, and it will take you through the very beginning of your goal until you reach success and achievement of those goals. If you decide not to be held back, you will not be and you'll never regret taking the first step of stepping into the water head first.

Day Sixteen

Dreams are interesting in that even when they're not really dreams, it's easy to think about how fast it's going to occur and how simple it'll be. You'll accomplish this just one thing, and someone will notice, and suddenly you're in the film with the famous actor. This could lead to believing that you don't know the things that it takes to be a successful worker for the goals you have set. I'm not saying that you are guilty of having thesethoughts, but it's the case that it is possible. Let's say you think it's easy but when you begin moving forward it becomes apparent the difficulty. This can be demotivating and lead you to decide to call your plans for the day. Be sure to resist the urge as long as you are able or that urge to go away from the right direction. Keep in mind how much you would like it, then consider how it could alter the way you live and give happiness. Consider it objectively and in smaller pieces. Instead of thinking about how huge the task is. Instead, take a look at the next steps. Yesterday , you opened the door and looked around. Then you took the first step. Now , you need to realize that it will not be an easy task. The most risky option for anyone who dreams as it can destroy the most beautiful of dreams and smother the brightest of stars. It can alter the outlook of the most determined man, and cause him to reconsider. You must be the limit of your ambitions 100% and totally. No matter how large or small, you must be determined, and don't let anything stop you from pursuing your goals. Day 16 is your chance to look the truth at the horizon, to be aware of how long the road is and to be elated. The harder the work is, the more successful. It is stated that nothing worthwhile is easy to achieve, and anything that is easily is worthy of having. Be prepared for the challenges of it. It is only better when you achieve it. Keep that in mind, and keep that thought in mind every time you're needed to.

Day Seventeen

If you're faced with a challenging travel, the idea of failure is likely to eventually come up. It's not something to be lost in or distracted by. However, it's a important thing to be aware of and aware. For a couple of specific reasons that can boost self-esteem. In the first place Failure is the sole way to be sure that you're taking the first steps toward something. Second, failing is to fail and that means you've got the confidence to begin any task. That is an aspect of success itself. While failure isn't an option for you, but it's an ongoing fact. If success is present is failure. There are two sides to one coin and will encounter both in your entire life. You don't really require me to explain this however, what you require to know is that it's acceptable to make mistakes. Failure without failure isn't as sweet. If the stakes weren't so high, nothing would merit fighting, and the tendency to be complacent would prevail. Human beings instinctively avoid failure, we run from it, run away from it, and we dislike it. It's not something we should be afraid of or hate, but rather to be afraid of or to. To be afraid of failing is to fear growing and the chance to learn. To be afraid of failing is to hate the lessons that the universe attempts to impart. To avoid failing is to stay away from the chance to become stronger and overcome obstacles. These are all crucial things to learn about. Without them, the achievement that we strive for wouldn't have its value. While you can't avoid the possibility of failure, you cannot stay away from it for the rest of your life. At some point , every person comes in contact with it. Today is the day to face the possibility of failing. Accept that it is there but resist the presence of it. Feel it, feel it and see it and most importantly acknowledge it. Day seventeen is in which we choose to achieve success. Take the failure as an opportunity to learn which will hinder your growth but do not let it hinder you from getting behind your goals. You'll fail many times in the path to success, but do not allow it to hinder your progress. In the end, your response to failure can affect your efforts in the future to achieve your objectives. Make sure you're able to manage failureand still be successful.

Day Eighteen

Once you've laid out your vision and made the initial steps, you're now able to begin thinking about long-term strategies for ensuring the success you've envisioned.. Start thinking about your plan for taking over and how you'll succeed. The last few days haven't been most pleasant. You've had to face the fear of failing and have pushed yourself to succeed to do something about it, and you've probably been scared all the time. This is a great thing. The thing they teach in their acting classes is that it's beneficial to embrace the discomfort. The same principle can be applied to the rest of your life. If you're scared of your decisions that you're in the best road. Therefore, it's time to persevere and truly focus on your goals. Be consistent, keep moving forward, and give 100% every step of the way. If you commit everything you have to something, it will be reciprocated ten times over. You must put all you can into what it is that you desire so that you can get back the money you have put into. It's always worthwhile as life is an investment and a lot of do not take the time to recognize that. Don't give less to yourself that you could as your future is contingent on it. Your present is only as long. With the commitment to a dream , your confidence in yourself has increased due to the determination and enthusiasm. Your self-esteem will increase your determination to achieve your desires and meet your goals. Therefore, approach it with the maximum amount of determination and never forget that you can achieve whatever you want to. Therefore, on the day of your 18th birthday decide to win and be determined to pursue your goals for regardless of how long it takes. Be steadfast and determined in the path you take Don't allow anyone to tell you contrary. Find your own motivation and continue to forge your path ahead and into the unexplored areas that make you fearful. Be strong and face the challenges that may arise. there's everything you'll need within you, and you're capable of doing anything. The most important thing is to be courageous and do your best.

Chapter 6: Rapid Increases Self-Esteem

Rituals are an excellent and effective way to increase confidence in yourself, but there are times when we require a increase throughout our day in order to keep up and going. You might be an individual with a high self-esteem however you require an extra boost to accomplish something crucial like an important business event. Perhaps you are trying to establish high self-esteem and would like to be awed prior to meeting an acquaintance. Whatever the case, it's important to learn how to increase your self-esteem when in the event of a crisis. This will help you to feel being confident and capable of conquering whatever you're facing.

The activities can be done in conjunction with an everyday self-esteem booster routine or employed to boost self-esteem at any given time or at any particular time. Incorporating these exercises into your self-esteem tools is a good option to ensure that you're able to boost yourself to be ready for anything and at any time. It is important to do them consistently to start to see the benefits and understand the ways they can benefit you. So, when you're in an emergency you'll know what to do and already be comfortable making use of them.

Power Poses

Power poses are an excellent method to boost confidence in yourself. They are specific poses designed to be performed in front of a mirror because being in these poses can give you an enormous boost to self-esteem. However, you can do them without a mirror if one does not be accessible when you require it. These poses are constructed in a manner that allows you to watch yourself performing confidence in your body language. This way, the exact response you feel when you observe another person who is practicing confident body language will be triggered. As you begin to connect this feeling with your own body, it becomes more easy to see you as the self-confident person. This boosts your self-esteem and you feel more confident with other people as well.

The most well-known exercises to practice is standing in front of a mirror , with your feet extended just a little beyond the width of your shoulders and with your arms raised in the shape of a "V" over your head, while holding your hands placed in fists. The pose is often referred to as "The Performer" and is believed to boost confidence and self-esteem because it makes you feel like you're winning. Because you appear as if you are part of the winning circle it is easy to believe that you have a lot of confidence. The pose is recommended to practice for at minimum 30 seconds, however it is generally recommended to keep it for an at least a minute to make the most of it. It can be boosted by saying affirmations to yourself when you hold the posture.

Exhaling your chest while keeping the hands placed on your hips, and placing your feet spaced hip-width apart is a excellent power stance. When we sit in this posture it gives us the impression that we're confident and in control. It's almost as if we are in a superhero pose and they feel proud of completing what they set out achieve. The act of standing in this position facing the mirror for 30-60 minutes, while saying affirmations to yourself is the perfect way to get used to it. You can also apply it in any circumstance that requires you to be more confident. For instance, if you are speaking with your manager, you could apply this pose. Be careful not to appear evident or awkward in your approach however, you should hold it steady and solid. In this way, you will be able to demonstrate your confidence to the world via your posture, while increasing your confidence within yourself by demonstrating it. This can help your confidence by making you appear more confident, while also feeling more confident.

Another one you can try is commonly referred to as"Superman Pose" or "Superman Pose." The Superman Pose is a good one to do in front of the mirror for about 30 to 60 minutes. It's as easy as standing in front of the mirror , with both feet set hip-width apart. placing one hand placed on your hip and the other extended above your head in the form of a fist. You can then raise your chest slightly and tilt your head upwards. This pose will make you feel powerful and strong, which can assist your belief that you are able to accomplish whatever you want to achieve.

Power poses are a great tool that can be practiced within a short amount of time to aid you in gaining a higher confidence. Although most of them are designed to be performed in an area with a mirror, or in the privacy of your own home but some are able to be practiced during a conversation to make your confidence to increase in the present moment. They're great in the event that you begin to see your self-esteem decline since they create an inner-body reminder that you're confident, capable and worthy. Understanding how you can use your body to relay this to your mind could help your confidence to rise when you are in the moment.

Posture

Our posture does not only speak volumes about who we are , but can have a significant influence on our perception of our self. People who dress in a slouchy, dragged-out manner or who attempt to make themselves appear smaller or more attractive by their posture are usually considered to be unfriendly and untrustworthy.

Being aware of your posture and knowing what it means not only to you, but also to others is vital. If your posture has been weakened and reduced in size There is a good likelihood that you're nervous and unsure about the circumstance you're in. This is an excellent indication of low self-esteem and confidence in oneself. Recognizing this in yourself is an excellent method to determine if you're expressing to yourself as well as to others around you that you are not confident. If you are able to tune into to this, it will also reveal to the cause of this anxiety within you. If you can feel your posture shift from a confident and capable posture to a timid and sluggish one, you'll be able to start to identify the cause and what caused it to cause your self-esteem to decline. If your posture always such, it might be because you've experienced low self-esteem over a period of time that you're struggling to feel at ease in any situation.

Assessing your posture is an excellent method to determine the problem, but it also gives you an opportunity to modify the way you stand. This way, you'll be able to start to develop a more energizing and more assured posture that demonstrates to others and yourself that you're a person with good self-esteem and a high level of self-confidence. It's some understanding about the way your posture and body language is perceived by yourself and other people.

A healthy confidence in oneself results in people who are in what is believed to be an ideal posture. This is having a straight, tall spine with a chin slightly rounded and feet that are well placed and hands comfortable or placed strategically in the body. For instance, placing your hands resting on your hips, with your arms laying on your sides or crossing your arms in front of you when you feel confident and confident. It is also important to keep your shoulders back, and keep your chest tucked slightly towards the front. This is thought as an ideal posture and one that is confident. If we are high and proud, we signal that we're feeling high and confident. This is then communicated to our brains, allowing us be more comfortable and proud .

Wardrobe

The way we dress can have significant influence on our mood and how we appear. If we dress badly it is likely that we will feel similar. If, for instance, you're wearing baggy, unfitting clothes, or ones that you don't feel comfortable in, then you're not likely to be confident. It will leave you feeling self-conscious, frustrated or even invisibly depending on the clothes you're wearing. All of these emotions do not can be equated to feeling confident or having a confidence in yourself.

The clothes you wear that fit well and feel great are crucial. You should wear clothes that feel comfortable on your skin, are well-fitting, and have a look that will make you feel comfortable and confident. If you dress in clothes that make you appear attractive, you are more comfortable when you wear them. It's no longer a time to be looking at your appearance in the mirror, or feeling self-conscious because of the fear of not looking good and not being noticed. not being noticed, thinking that there's something wrong with your outfit that may make you embarrassed. Instead, you're able to be focused on other aspects of your life.

If you're currently wearing an outfit that doesn't inspire you to feel that you are confident to assert yourself at any time You should start altering your wardrobe! Comfortable clothes for lounging is essential, but you must ensure that your wardrobe is not comprised of the same. Also, don't pick clothes solely on the basis of their label. If the style doesn't feel appropriate for you Don't purchase it. Instead, focus on creating your ideal appearance: Match what feels and looks right for you. For instance, let's say you're looking professional, but you don't like jackets. You might instead find the perfect style of dress or blouse shirt that flatters you and helps you feel more confident. Instead of filling your wardrobe with blazers that are well-fitting that cause you to look at yourself with disgust or resentment, dress yourself in stylishly-fitting dresses or blouses that will make you feel confident and confident.

A well-constructed wardrobe implies that it has items for all occasions. Finding the perfect item of clothing for any type of occasion will ensure that you'll always look at your best, in a manner that makes you feel good every time.

If you're not sure what you should wear to look and feel fabulous You might want to consider hiring stylists. Talking to someone who can assist you in deciding on what look is appropriate and how you will look and feel great wearing it is an excellent method to create an outfit that can boost confidence in yourself. In addition, it is useful if you've not shopped before and don't know which items to buy yourself. Also having stylists cheer you on to tell how amazing you are in the new pieces might be the perfect thing you require to feel comfortable wearing after you purchase. This will ensure that the pieces don't get to your closet and not be worn due to the fear of wearing them out of fear of lack of self-confidence.

Assertiveness

Making yourself known isn't always straightforward however it is vital. People who are self-conscious struggle to assert their self-worth and result in feeling unrepresented and exploited in various situations. If others don't know what you're thinking or how strongly your feelings are about specific issues and issues, they're not going to be able take your words seriously. In addition, there are some who don't know how be taken seriously by others unless they are forced to do it by another person's assertiveness. Learning to assert yourself will not only make others consider you a serious person, but it can also assist you to learn how to be treated with respect.

People who aren't used to assertiveness may be influenced by a false notion of what assertiveness actually is. This is usually due to the fear of being perceived as a threat and misunderstanding. A lot of people who don't exercise assertiveness may believe that doing so is being rude and arrogant with regards to your beliefs and thoughts. It's not the case. Although asserting yourself is handled in a gentle and respectful manner but it still needs to have an impact that is powerful and positive. The reason you assert yourself isn't to sound loud and inconsiderate instead, you should remain firm and consistent. It is important to ensure that others are aware of what you are feeling and they know that you will keep asserting your position until they are able to comprehend or accept.

It is crucial to assert yourself in ensuring that your needs are taken care of and also in getting your thoughts and opinions heard when they should be. For instance, let's say that in a relationship you are not happy that someone has to wait for you without notifying you. If you don't ever assert that this is not acceptable for you, and that you don't like waiting around, particularly without prior notice, the other party won't notice and will not be pressured to change their approach. Or, they might know when you've made a statement on occasion but they won't consider you a serious person since you don't back the assertion with a strong argument.

Let's suppose that you have clearly stated to them that you are not happy that they're tardy. You also state to them that, in the near future you'll just not sit around. Then, you quit and quit the next time they make the mistake. They will be able to see from the sequence of events that you're serious. It is a way of asserting your self.

Another excellent scenario in which you can make a difference by making yourself known is in a professional environment. For instance, suppose you're at the board room. The board is set to take action that will result in you taking on more responsibility, but you're not able effectively manage the work within your timetable. Being able to state that you're not comfortable to take on the additional work , and stating your preferred solution is an excellent method to ensure that you're not being exploited and to ensure that your requirements and those of the business remain fulfilled. The ability to assert yourself comes in handy at many times. Believing in yourself and your beliefs is essential, so make certain to practice it. The more you exercise assertiveness more, the more natural and comfortable it becomes to be able to do it anywhere and when you're required to.

Chapter 7: Reducing Your Anxiety Levels

This is a concern for people from all different walks of life. If you discover a way to reduce anxiety, this will allow you go through your day in a positive manner. Positive attitude can increase confidence in yourself. So, I would like you to complete the exercises described in this section on a regular basis. The reason you should do it each day, no matter if you think it's helping you is because it's becoming an habit that replaces some of the bad habits that led you to anxiety.

Let me explain. There are two components of your brain. There are the conscious thoughts that you make every day, which triggers an emotional reaction to the events in your life and then there is the subconscious mind. This is the most clever part of the brain which records your reactions will be to your surroundings. If you cry when you spot an animal, your subconscious mind is convinced that your response is a fight or flight, and so each time you come across mice, your stress levels will increase. This is the way you react. The thing that scientists have discovered is that you can change this negative response that your subconscious has recorded and change it into positive reactions. So, for instance, every whenever you see the mouse, you smile and dance around in a circle and then forget about the fear and will begin recording your new response. Of course, I'm not here to help with fears. I was just trying to explain this to make sure you understand the process.

If you're in the public space, perhaps you feel anxious. You might feel sweaty or you don't know how to handle the situation. If you're struggling with self-esteem and you are facing the situation in a manner which could hurt your self-esteem more. If, for instance, you've suffered from a negative experience with your spouse, you might think that you don't deserve more respect than that even if you decide to leave your spouse, there is a chance that you'll be drawn to another person who is similarly abusive. Why? Because you've built your mind up to accept this to be an expected reaction from being you. It's not a normal response however, what's taking place will be what is known as the Law of Attraction. You present yourself to the world as a victim, and the only person you're likely to attracted to is one who loves victims and therefore will dominate your. You present yourself as a confident and confident person and everything changes. You will attract happy and confident people who enrich your life rather than taking away from it.

I am awed by the way that I explain how to reduce anxiety since it works each time. The key is in the way you breathe to some degree. When you're nervous or uncertain and confidence, you may not breathe correctly and then there is an accumulation of excessive oxygen within your blood stream, leading to fear. This is the body's reaction in response to the breath you take. So, if you are able to are able to control your breathing it will aid you greatly as you'll be in control during those times which normally cause you to be extremely nervous.

The first exercise is breathing properly

I would like you to sit on a firm backed chair and set your feet upon the flooring. Your back should be straight, as you might not even be aware of it, however, you do have vital points in the spine region. If they're restricted by poor posture, they could cause you many problems. Then, inhale through your nostrils, and exhale out. I'd bet you breathed in approximately 3 counts. Humans do this. They are prone to breathe in enough, and as you become more and more stressed, you are breathing at a slower pace, taking in greater amounts of oxygen that you require. Take a deep breath and count up to 6. Then try it again to 7. The concept is to count up to seven and then exhale until you've reached 10. Why do you exhale more air that you inhale? It helps to restore the level that oxygen is in the bloodstream. this can help you ease into your sleep.

It is possible to do this exercise routine for 15 minutes every morning when you get up, or when you arrive home at night, before you consume food. Don't do it on an empty stomach. Try to do it in the same timeframe every day. It is also possible to use it throughout the day when you encounter situations that cause anxiety and you begin to feel more calm because you're not taking in too much oxygen and you aren't putting your body in anxiety mode.

Exercise 2 - Allow yourself time to relax

This exercise proves that you are entitled to perform something you like doing every moment of the day. It doesn't matter if you're one who enjoys relaxing in a bath or listening to the music they love isn't important. You decide. The time you spend with yourself will help you realize that you have the right to rest and what makes you feel relaxed is acceptable. Perhaps a stroll in the countryside, or reading an ebook. Whatever you decide to do, dedicate fifteen minutes every day, even if it involves reading your favourite book at the sink! You're worthy of it, and it will help you increase your self-esteem and have less anger since you can't find the enough time to complete the tasks you'd like to. You have the right to take care of yourself, and it's not selfish at all. If you feel great about yourself, then take it on.

Chapter 8: Block Negative Waves

"We tend to focus on a significant area of the province that, in my opinion is the cause of chaos as well as fear and negative energy throughout the world. I believe that if we concentrated on what is common to us and what we'd all be content," according to DeGeneres Ellen The world would be a better place for us to be nice to all . People who consider you blessed to be focused more on the things that matter to them. It is possible to accomplish your goals when you are blessed. " For all other dreamers, don't attempt to keep from doing it or with a negative perspective when you look at the world or even be embarrassed, you are the divine spirit of God. Because you've believed in yourself and loved yourself as well and as many people as you can - Adam Green says. Adam Green about breaking positive thinking to rid yourself of negative waves. However, you're in the middle of attempts to cause people to produce negative outcomes. Contrarian opinions are infectious. If you haven't found the right people and love like Adam suggested that the harmful green waves strike. The person may experience problems with services. "Have you recently overcome the test of your life and broken with someone you love? If yes, it's crucial to take into consideration the time frame after each incident that the person who suffered the injury is the lion's tame in order to manage the negative power that could attack you in the future. ? Aristotle Salmansohn. Never more than once do waves strike the negative energy that holds your life on the ship.

Take lessons the lessons of Quinones Miller Cornelius. And he added, "and when they say to me:" I won't do it, "they don't pretend, that they aren't able to do, which is to say that they cannot collaborate together." Not by the company. If you're insole, they've completed the project. A proud pessimist who is always in need of all to be seen by him. This is why it will be beneficial to the community. It's unlikely to make them accessible to you. You must find your clients who are definitely at the top of the same inborn. Accounts are in charge of your mobile lives and individuals aren't. The stroke's wave function is dangerous because you are trying to live your life. The writer Martin Buber affirms that once again, but it's an opinion. In the end, m stops pungency from being favorable to the return motion. " This means that you're as a natural part of the other. There are no work-related issues for them and you are able to accept the idea. And" Opeur If not they are in agreement with the destiny. What? Do not touch or touch anything that desecrates the desecration of faith in the negative and are not doing so take precautions and to keep the subject from this way to reach. "The negative energy is a cannibal. This makes it larger and more difficult to feed" Darnell Earnings reports. Darnell Income reports. The age of old is what results from negative thoughts that are not distinct from the other. I believe Dahnke is right. Dahnke would like them to understand that a lot of people do not believe in the statements of gods who are positive when they are at lowest point and are unable to see the negative. Hello people do not improve. To meet more challenges, what and that is not damaged, is possible? This should not be a part of the lifestyle and culture of negativity and opposition.

"People are more likely to speak negative words to lower self-esteem. I feel sorry for myself and it is a reflection of their thoughts is the negative is apparent. Hendrie writes. Weisinger People who have low self-esteem do not have any problems in their lives. What is the reason people are so smug? There must always be timid fear. "Some begin to transform the course of their life for good. John

O'Donohue would like you to be aware that "addiction is now counting with the rest of us who reside on the left side in darkness ... Eliminating negative thoughts, and transforming negative thoughts isn't feasible, and directing it towards the shining light of their souls. " Thus, positive actions negative effects of wine. Don't focus on the negatives. Consider some suggestions that will help you to improve your life. Because it's Ambika Wauters, all negativity is not the result of the mind created thing is limited, therefore I will defend and protect it. Do you not think that those with limitations aren't in disbelief of the nature of life's waves. The passage was simple with the strongest but also damaging waves. I am awestruck that MacLaine admitted to school, which cannot be negative. His words: "That will not only confirm his dwelling in the power of his mind." It is the presence of oxygen. Refusal to believe that it been dead this spring. Cicero Francis knew what he stated: "the reduction in November will be the same as the failure that was expected." Negative deficits as a different objective. If you are successful on the front, just breath in space.

To Mark Twain, the writer, "terrible listening only is not a good thing for a son." To end this deplorable situation, Masaaki Hatsumi this warning that he is "ignorant about the pain or anger, hatred and illegality that doesn't cause him any discomfort. Nearly the harsh breeze has gone. It's not going to happen again. This is a crime. This person didn't experience the profound sensation of this side, happiness and joy in Life that Challenges! for the negative wave of Min East Challenges that assist develop. Are they on? Alphonse Karr who states that "no need to complain about the thorns" Carrera We thank God for roses that have thorns. Negativity isn't just an article, but rather the concept was derived from it. Do not stop any potential negative situations to make a decision. Smith willtem Please let those who have nothing to do and your mind was upset. " You! It's your life! and what do we talk about? You must be a realist. Do not make assumptions about other people derived by your experience. Don't be concerned about things. If there is something bad, they are able to stop the flow of negative results. This is not surprising considering that this is the case with Dr. Anil K Sinha "Ansieta the length of time it takes to build a fortress and is a lot more than the truth. " advertising negative aspects of lifedue to confusion and achieve what nalozysz wave at developers.

Based on Brian Tracy, "a Credibility Positive affirmation of harm or beneficial in the afternoon to make a decision about what you're doing and how to do it." There's nothing to wake up from, or to PIU which is, I believe that the qualities it has within it. Therefore you are unable to believe in it, it's not possible to suggest that we do not trust in the inherent capabilities. "If you believe in the power of technology, there are likely bring about negatives on your personal life. You can see the bad and positive.

However you must think that it is positive thoughts to discover the root of the positive mind , according to Byron Pulsifer. If waves are not harmful, then A issue. According to the experts, the most effective one that is affected by its qualification quality is to say it is the case that. However, if you feel that it will not grow, you won't be competent to assist you in your current situation. Was sent, but not it was a forced negative. To be 'begotten', to be capable of believing. Vivamus desire to understand the Smith "either is referring to the works , and particularly those that are positively positive or negative are removed. " Nothing can increase the limits of the universe, unless you are unjust and who puts himself in his place. " It's always happened every thing that is positive are positive. It's as simple as taking two glances. If not, fill your thoughts with positive thoughts but also with negative thoughts as in the Empedocles Abderitesque Ali. This is the court. How he would like to play. Keep in mind that this is your life and be clear about where you're going. However, before taking a decision one step at a time, more important take a moment to hail John would like them to understand that "no one is able to be positive in a negative for the continual utilization of the word."

"Fear of denial inside a small , dark room" as portrayed by Michael Otto Fabrice. Don't be distracted by the latest concerns. Better to get furniture, and then it will follow! The fear of the enemy is everything good in our souls of the human race. It is imperative to feel fear strike something significant for me to last a lifetime! George Baker wants to know about every person, and what's becoming apparent as a sign of the end. " In this way that he might need to shout always, but when everything will hit the waves and negative energy. In lieu of screaming, or an opposite , God has provided strength to strike into the dough as well as your waves. From this perspective, it should comprehend that might be to perceive the distance property that can accommodate, it is necessary to worship. Control your understanding. Concentrate on your God to do. Keep in mind that, as per the Bhagavad Gita, "the enemy of the soul lives in the same situations as someone who is not limited by it." He enticed the mind of the king and then he formed the places that alter the life's circumstances. Take lessons by them. But do don't allow your soul to manage them. Steve Maraboli. The same plane has to stop diluting thoughts or ideas or pollute away. " Instead, it could be that you were living. In addition, it's not weighed down by the results of your actions as of yet! Iyanla Vanzant's research because there is a sense of proud that they are more than all of them. In reality, "this" is different and is repeated with you when you are not to you. That means the actions of people who are not superior to yours. You must focus on yourself and the determination you have to follow the goal one step at a time.

Deepika demonstrates how it can be a catalyst for the recognition of the fruit of our lives. He also said: " I am not an account, but and it's not in the negatives that it does not regret. It is true that at an era, it will leave the Sent to improve however, it eventually gets exhausted of. It is not with you. He is easily forgotten and forgiven and forgive, which will be all to do it. will please you. And peace offering. " Hugh Dillon says that you should not use devices that are detrimental, since "life can be too brief to dwell with negativity." Dillon said: "I made a conscious attempt to not become what people want to be."

There is no one who feels like the pessimists since it was the norm to be successful in life or have value. Alesha Dixon wishes people to understand that "when you think about the harm that occurs for us and the consequences it is for us, we're probably not being triggered in the face take a look at the issue, and shift our thinking in order to lessen the negative. His area of concern in the conditions of departure from the exit could be just one. If he could only ascend by the hand of the lady in love and the object is lost! Should I do something? What are you looking for in some kind of word. You have to point to you! This is He the way that you are able to change your life and all the goodness that it brings. You, not the negative is what you should turn. "Focus your energy, work and. Movement and conversation with people can help to encourage culture and be pleasant. You'll also feel more confident and witty when "The author Marco Tulio said Salmansohn. The advice of years was that one shouldn't" fire in the negativity and positive energy that seeks to fulfill the an intention or desire for and I have done. Sometimes, I've added to the list that I have done things for my family Sometimes I fight to protect my friends.

"People tend to sharing their successes and losses insignificant pigs, and are fearful of being ignorant. Slight seems negative. Protein diets that are rich in memory use this type of movement. You can keep your entire life away free of the soul food choices, and your soul. A decisive push that's positive for me. Refill paliwowi, says Steve Maraboli when they do. The danger of negative range even in the society. I've tried outdoor cams on guard against people who are enthralled by life and irritating because they have reason you're dead. " These men cause harm. " He has MIT MIT and his Life. Israelmore Ayivor would like them to be aware that their thoughts are able to carry their thoughts -the ability to be tired of technology! Create a football relationship that can discern what is being seen as well as what is and isn't it will help to help them develop plans to put into place. Cicero Stephen explained that "not always eliminate negative thoughts, and without iron-to iron fighting, but to it, you could be able to dominate them, which means there's no fruit, follow me. " Do what you can to make them in as negative a manner as I would like to, ends in the raging waters in the prison. It's a little surprise Asmaa Dokmak declares" regarding the construction industry, they are not afraid that an opposing opinion could change. In the end, Bernadette Dimitrov would like to know "If we be surrounded by destructive thoughts or harmful ideas and harmful thoughts, then we'll not be able to maintain it and will probably be unsatisfied with it."

Chapter 9: Self-Esteem Deterioration Can Cause Self-Harm

Self-harm

Self-harm refers to the act of deliberately injuring yourself, typically with the intention of decreasing. A person can injure themselves to alleviate psychological stress.

Self-injuring behaviors are not the same as an attempt to destroy yourself. People who self-harm may attempt self-destruction, but in the main self-harming actions, they do not indicate a desire to live a life that is not.

The treatment can help those who are looking to end NSSI. If you or a loved one is having a problem and you are in need of help, seek out emergency assistance. Contact the National Suicide Prevention Lifeline at 1-800-273-8255 and talk to someone whenever you can.

What is the term "SELF-HARM?

Self-injury may occur in many forms:

70 70% to 90% of NSSI behaviors involve reducing the method by which one cuts only superficially within their skin. The majority of non-suicidal cuts are performed on the wrists because of the possibility of rupturing the capillary.

21-44% of all scenarios involve hitting the head or throwing yourself against a wall.

15 to 35 percent of those who suffer from self-harm, shed skin, usually by lighting a suit or smoking cigarettes.

Self-embedding can be a serious type of self-harm where the victim inserts objects directly in their skin, like staples or needles. The item could remain in place for an entire time or even for a time period of collection.

One could be involved in various self-harming activities at the same time of time. The most frequent locations to inflict harm on oneself is the wrists, hands as well as the belly and upper legs.

CAUTION SIGNS OF SSELF-HARM

Self-harm sufferers frequently try to hide their behavior from their peers. They also tend to record their actions. Here are some signs that an individual may be hurting themselves

Injuries that are not considered to be serious: A person may have frequent swellings or cuts that they denounce to "crashes. ".

The stockpile of equipment A person could have a number of sharp objects which appear to have no purpose, like containers or needles. Additionally, they may be subject to various razors that are not common.

Blood discolorations on items Self-harm actions could tarnish a person's towels, clothing or bed linens. A person could also have many bloody bandages or tissues in their trash.

Covering clothing: One may wear long sleeves or pants to hide marks, and also in the heat.

Insularity: A person could lock themselves away in a room or shower for prolonged time to harm themselves by committing self-harming. They may also withdraw from social activities in general.

Self-harming individuals could have issues functioning in the office or at an institution. The battle they face to manage their emotions can cause problems for their relationships. They could also display lower self-esteem.

A person who exhibits one of these signs could or may have self-injuries. The visible presence of many signs, however it is likely to be a cause for concern. If you're concerned about your loved one You can discuss your circumstances with a situation person via the National Suicide Prevention Lifeline: 1-800-273-8255.

What is the reason people choose to self-harm?

A lot of people use self-harm as a way to cope for mental confusion. Self-injury can serve a variety of purposes at different instances. People who self-injure could be trying to:.

Feel uncomfortable Self-harm sufferers might be unable to communicate their feelingsor may have feelings that culture blocks their from expressing. Some people may use NSSI to release a stress they are unable to confront.

Distract themselves: Some may find physical discomfort easier to handle than a temper or isolation. Physical discomfort can help people to focus on the present rather than their current situation.

The person might feel shameful for the perceived issue or a sense of guilt due to a previous mistake. Self-harm could be seen as the only way to reduce these feelings.

Feel pleasure: Injuring your flesh can cause the body to release pain-reducing chemical substances known as Narcotics. The "feel-good" compounds can cause an effective, but brief sensation of high.

Feel like you have a sense of control: People who suffered a serious injury (particularly the sexual violence) may feel vulnerable following the reality. NSSI may be an approach to regain control over their emotions and body.

Feel anything at all: Many people who self-harm report feeling physically as if they are numb. They could use NSSI to tell themselves how they live a life of.

All kinds of self-harm use physical discomfort in order to treat mental problems. The relief that self-harm can provide for some individuals is only temporary. Self-harm may prevent individuals from developing more secure, safer self-harming devices.

The course of self-harm.

Often, people experience anxiety and stress. This is triggered to by the desire to self-harm. The person is likely to engage self-harm to relieve the anxiety. They may feel embarrassed about participating the NSSI as well as the marks caused due to the habit.

Self-harm can be a result of the same kind of program associated with alcohol and drug dependence, which is accompanied by secrets and routines. The person may want to end the behaviors, but feel in a position to not be able to. One could think that wounding themselves is the only way to ease their suffering.

Certain people who hurt themselves will take great care to prevent severe injuries or infections. Self-harm, whether it is regular or not, can be a danger to the health of an individual's well-being, as well as the degree to which they are functioning.

Self-Harm and Suicide.

Self-harming actions aren't kind of self-destructive behaviors. NSSI is generally a means to live life and not to complete it. It is possible for people to feel dull and use the pain of self-injury as a way to convince themselves that they can live their lives.

A persistent self-harming habit can put one at risk of becoming self-destructive in the near future. A study from 2011 estimates more than fifty percent of those who engage in self-harm have attempted self-destruct in the past.

Even if injuries aren't serious self-harming actions can be dangerous. Self-harm could increase the chance of deliberate and unintentional death. The treatment for NSSI may eventually save the life of a person.

DATA SUR the SELF-HARM

Self-injury could begin at any age. However Most people who self-harm are teenagers or young adults. In Western countries, self-injury typically starts between 13 and 15 years of age. The United States, self-injury happens in the following categories:

-- 1.3 percent of children between 5 and 10 years old.

17% of teenagers

15% of university students (some research studies indicate 35 percent).

4.4% of the adult population.

Self-harm behavior differs widely by country. The average life-time frequency of university students differs between 10 percent within Japan to 38 percent in Indonesia. In general, the factors that result in self-injury (misuse or anxiety, other factors) are common to all society.

Aged people of various age and ethnic backgrounds queue at the airport's terminal. Numerous studies have shown that Native Americans are at boosted danger of self-harm, and African-Americans seem to be more protected.

Research suggests that about 35 percent of Americans who self-harm are men. Females are the most likely to cut themselves.

A study conducted in 2012 found 18 percent of LGBTQ+ high schoolers engaged self-harm. Researchers suggest that sex-related minorities could employ self-harm in order to cope with the pressure of preconceptions as well as fear.

Tips to avoid self-harm.

There is a chance that you or someone whom you are familiar with cut themselves. Top-end celebs such as Angelina Jolie as well as Demi Lovato have actually cut and have helped bring awareness about the issue through telling their stories of recovery.

Self-harm is much more common than you realize, with a recent finding that as much as 46 percent of students in senior high schools have been involved at some point. Reduced self-harm has been found to be so prevalent, that even as a professional I've heard girls complain at me about how it's so typical Some feel that people won't take their thoughts seriously unless they also take part in the activity.

What exactly is reducing? This is a non-adaptive method of dealing with issues that involve self-inflicting discomfort that is not suicide by cutting, using anything from fingernails or razors or shedding their own hair, or avoiding past injuries to be healed. There are numerous reasons why people engage in these dangerous habits as a way to manage extreme emotions or as a method of "sensation" in the event that a person is feeling like they are numb, to control. Teenagers typically define the feeling of reduction as being happy, or experiencing a sensation of a launching. It is likely to be due to the increased levels of endorphins that are released by the brain when reducing the appearance of the size of the skin.

It is crucial to first realize that reducing weight does not actually solve any kind of problem and isn't an effective method of dealing with issues with issues that will last. The feeling of a rush that comes from the reduction of weight is temporary and doesn't address the underlying issue that causes the sensation or lack of feeling which is the reason for the behavior in the first place. Additionally, there is an unfavorable connection the self-harm process as well as self-destructing efforts.

If you have reduced the amount you cut, it's possible to stop. The trick is to change the behavior using a healthy, well-balanced coping system.

Find the triggers.

You can ask yourself to determine if there are any specific circumstances or circumstances which make you appear to be decreasing (i.e. times of day, periods or specific topics)? This could be helpful to discuss together with another person.

Determine feelings.

How do you feel prior to or after you decide to cut back? (I.e. disoriented, anxious, misinterpreted (i.e. lonesome, dispirited, nervous, confused, etc. on) How long will the feeling last before you want to decrease it once more?

Tell someone.

The process of reducing is typically an event that is extremely private and you could conceal and even attempt. Let a friend know that could use a helping hand or even be an on board for the information you're doing.

Seek out assistance from a professional.

Consult your physician or hospital registered nurse psychologist, or psychoanalyst each of them can help you or direct you to someone who will provide a customized therapy. Reduced levels could be an indication (such as that of the Borderline Personality Disorder) or be a result of a mental health issue (such as anxiety or eating disorders). Working with a professional will help you not only to recognize the signs, but also help you learn to be more in control of your mind.

Try a more moderate type.

It is best to do this under the supervision of an expert, however it is possible to look at less invasive methods to get similar relief until you can use more effective methods of coping. (For example taking off an elastic band, or placing an ice cube in your hands.) In the end it will be to shift to more self-soothing activities like writing, exercise and art, pursuing a non-judgmental vanity, relaxing in a comfortable bathroom and savoring every now and then a reward, and so on.

Write letters to yourself for the future.

" It is easy to come up with healthy and well-balanced strategies to deal with psychological stress even when you're doing good, but it can be really difficult when it's 4 a.m. and your world is crumbling," keeps in mind the medical psychotherapist Dana Harron, PsyD. "For this reason I have young clients whom I work with to write notes and lists of strategies for dealing with their future 4 a.m. selves.' In certain instances they can create 'open letters like "open when you feel terrible, "open when you truly feel left out etc while they're in the healthy and balanced zone. ".

Postpone.

Begin by counting and then try to get to reach 100 and examine if the desire persists after you have felt the need to cut. If you are able, remove yourself from the space or situation that you are in and also observe whether the urge lingers after you've gotten off by yourself. In the end, you could increase the time you put off it and change the actual cutting down with a healthy, appropriate coping strategy.

Consider Dialectical Treatment for Behavior.

It is a form that is a form of modification to the cognitive behaviour which is used to help people who are self-destructive or who suffer from borderline personality disorder and self-injure themselves. As per the National Alliance on Mental Health:.

DBT differs from conventional CBT in its emphasis on recognition. It is an effective method that lets both the person and the professional work on "approving" uncomfortable thoughts, actions and sensations rather of having difficulty working with the ideas, actions and sensations. If a certain thought, feeling or idea have been confirmed that the process of adjustment is no longer challenging, and the objectives of progressive changes become a reality.

Increase your mindful.

Try to stay present in the moment and remain in the present. Encourage yourself to return to the present moment with a gentle and non-judgmental manner if you notice your thoughts wandering off or engaging in self-deflection.

You can feel the launch.

Find a place that is personal and discover a launch point by shouting. Let the aggression and force to flow and be able to feel the launch.

Remain favorable.

Learn and try stories of success to motivate you on the path to recovery. It is possible to recover, though the journey may be difficult. You'll definitely become more confident when you're done.

Chapter 10: Different Techniques To Build Self Esteem

Method 1: Take a Record of Your Self-Esteem

Pick up a piece or paper, and trace a line across the middle. On the top, you should label the first column "Strengths" and the other column 'Weaknesses'. Then, list 10 items for each column. The aim in this task is to provide you with the idea as to what may have to do to conquer your self-esteem issues. If you have a low self-esteem, you may find it difficult to think of 10 items. If that's the case, consider referring to the compliments others have made to you. Remember that you may not always perceive yourself in a clear way, especially in the case of self-esteem issues.

When you've got your list of strengths, go through it and be sure that you have the capabilities. These are things you can build blocks to develop other abilities. They also represent the things you already excel at in the real world. Even when you feel down in yourself have the strengths you can draw on.

While you go through the list of flaws take note that you're looking at a an array of things you can improve about yourself. There's no one trait that is not changeable with effort. This is also true in the development of new abilities. When you're ready to work hard you are able to accomplish whatever you want to. Select at least one item from your list of flaws you'd like to improve on. Set goals and establish goals. In time, you'll be able to shift this weakness into your strengths column.

Technique 2: Put Life into Perspective

Do you believe that people be able to remember about you once you're gone and dead? Do you think they'll be sat around talking about the moment you made a mistake during a talk or fell on the book in the air? Most likely, they won't. It's easy to lose our sense of self-confidence when we think people are making fun of us for our shortcomings even though they have not spoken about it. It is essential to remember that the majority of people don't look at you with such a keen eye. If they did notice that you made a mistake during the presentation, they'll forget about it towards when they have finished the day, or even at the conclusion of the presentation. They're not likely to be sitting around for the rest of the weekend, joking about how fell at work.

It is true that people don't pay enough focus on life as much as we believe they are, especially our coworkers or acquaintances who we don't have a close relationship with. They're focussed on their personal objectives and their own life. That means that if you are tempted to blame yourself for making a mistake, the majority of people won't even be able to recall the incident. Consider a moment to think about the future and speak to yourself. If you look at your life from a different angle What will come up? Does that really going to be important? It's easy to create an entire mountain from the molehill when you are involved personally. In the overall world of things these moments are pointless. Let it go and get on with your life.

Technique 3. Do the most difficult thing on your To-Do List first.

Some tasks are daunting when you consider the entire process. For instance those who work in the week may spend weekends doing chores around the home. If their agenda is full of chores, like cleaning the gutters, scrub the bathtub, sweep the floors, or take away the garbage It can be very easy to delay things that they would like to get done. But, when the sun goes down and they've not completed the most difficult task to do, it appears to have been wasted.

Instead of delaying those things you don't want to tackle until the end take them done first. The person mentioned above could tackle getting rid of the gutters the first. This will not only take the longest time, but it's also an ideal time to start when there is daylight outside. Also, by clearing your gutters before you do, the most difficult task is out of way and everything else is to be a breeze.

4. Take care of yourself

If you truly love anyone, will you give them junk food, force them to stay in bed until late at evening, or urge them to curl up on the couch rather than be active? Absolutely not. The most significant aspect of developing confidence in yourself is learning how to take good care of yourself. You can't rely on others to take care of your life. You must ensure you're doing what is right. One of the reasons people gain weight is that they lack confidence in themselves to care for themselves. They persist with their unhealthy habits as they are unwilling to change, or don't believe they are entitled to a better standard of living. The importance of taking care of yourself affects your mental health. It is essential to take time to appreciate your hard work completed and to relax. Be kind to yourself and take a break every now and then. If you are pushing yourself too hard your mind will eventually fail.

The issue with failing to look after your self properly is that it can lead to an upward slope that leads to lower self-esteem. If you don't take care of your diet and exercise routine and exercise, it could lead to physical health problems or obesity. These, in turn can cause low self-esteem. Also, not getting sufficient sleep can impact your mental and emotional health as well as cognitive capabilities. This can affect self-esteem as well in the sense that you feel you are unable to control your thoughts or aren't capable of accomplishing the work you have to. If you don't make enough breaks during your work, you might feel petty about yourself because you are unable to think clearly.

Don't allow unwholesome habits to harm your self-esteem, show yourself affection. Make sure you nourish your body with appropriate foods and stay away from things that can harm your body. Be responsible and have enough self-love to fall asleep in the right time so you'll be able to get up the next morning and have the greatest chances of being at ease and achieving your goals. Give yourself time to relax and relax. Being aware that you deserve these indulgences will make you realize that you are worthy of the self-love you fail to show yourself from time to time.

Technique 5: Look at Criticism as an opportunity to grow

Individuals who have low self-esteem or confidence could be looking too closely at criticism. They might view it as a thing they must improve on, and it could make someone already feeling depressed. Instead of seeing criticism as negative, take this as an opportunity for growth. Be aware that there isn't one person on earth who is flawless. There are flaws and flaws that make them distinct. Furthermore negative feedback is crucial in determining what changes you'd like to change. If you don't know what's wrong you will not be able to implement positive changes.

But, it's important to keep in mind that some feedback may not be constructive. If a coworker, boss or a friend has a tendency to speak negatively regarding you and helping to get better isn't their primary goal. The constant criticism they offer is best avoided, since it comes from a negative source.

Technique 6: Be Grateful

It's easy to get caught up in negative feelings when you don't take the time to take time to appreciate the things in your life. By taking time each day to notice what's going well in your life, you're showing self-love. You also give yourself the opportunity to see that not everything that happens in your life is bad. There are plenty of positive experiences and things in your life to be thankful for. It doesn't matter what it is, being awake each day and being able to rest in food and a warm home for the return trip when you get home from work are things you should be thankful for.

Be grateful for what you have. Keep a notebook in your bag throughout your day. If you experience something that is positive take note of it. Make a point of identifying at least three positive items each day that are thankful for. Remember that you'll notice these things more if you're paying attention when you are going through your day. You won't be able to appreciate the blossoming flowers that mark the beginning of spring if you're making plans for your day prior to heading to work.

Technique 7: Stop Expecting Perfection

The notion of perfection is both unattainable and damaging to self-esteem. One reason people become angry when they don't have everything flawless is because they are living believing that other people are perfect. Have you met someone you know who never seemed to fail to make mistakes? They always look amazing and always meet deadlines, and do not dispute with colleagues. Be aware that many people don't celebrate their errors. They're not in the office talking about how they delayed their work over the weekend and needed to stay up late working on their work. Instead, they remain calm and focused. They appear as if they completed the task Friday night and then enjoyed all weekend enjoying themselves.

Even when everything appears perfect, they aren't always. Everyone has mistakes. They are just not always making them known. People are not happy being viewed as flawed, despite the fact that imperfections are a normal part of life. Although it is difficult to be perceived as flawed in social situations, you must stop thinking that you can be perfect. Be aware that you're only human, just like those around you. Although you may not acknowledge their mistakes, they exist.

Technique 8: Make a Difference

One of the main reasons many people feel that they're lacking in life is due to their own personal circumstances. If you are living solely by yourself, it may be difficult to discern what you are worth independent of the business you work for or even at your home. One method to overcome an unmotivated state is to engage in something important. Send care packages or letters to soldiers who don't have families or work at your nearby animal shelter, or soup kitchen. Bring a trash bag to the woods or to the beach to pick up garbage. If you do something such as this for other people and help them, it makes an impact on the way you perceive your worth as an individual.

If you feel that your schedule is to be a bit occupied with these charitable events, try being kind. When you show kindness to those in your life, it will make an important change in how you are viewed by others. Being kind is also an effective step that can set off an entire sequence of events in motion. The events that occur can prompt others who are around you to be nice towards you, too. If you can see that you're worthy of kindness from others You may also come to realize that you deserve your own kindness.

Technique 9: Keep in Mind Your Self-Worth Is Not measured by performance

Many people see life as a race. They are determined to achieve the highest marks in whatever they try. But, if they're defeated by someone who is superior than them, it could be damaging to self-esteem. This is due to the fact that it is very simple to connect the actions you do with the worth you feel as an individual.

It is a fact that you can't use your achievements done to determine your self-worth. Each person has a journey. They have different success levels. It could be because the person who did well been more disciplined or they were more prepared. What is more important than performance is the desire to take a risk. Every time you decide to try something new, you're taking a step outside your comfortable zone. This alone can make you a successful person.

Technique 10: Express Your Insecurities

Technology has accomplished a lot of great things for humanity. However, it has made it more difficult to maintain relationships. Consider the last time you went out with a friend and they were constantly on their phones all the duration. Didn't you feel neglected? The thing to consider in this scenario is that the person who has been neglected might not be aware that your habits on the phone are causing problems for you. In addition, many people view their phones as a form of addiction. They constantly check it since it's become their routine.

Instead of expressing anger at the person you're having a conversation with, it's essential to communicate what you feel. Be sure that you let it be known to that person who is causing trouble for you. Most people will find this is enough to get them to drop the phone and show you the attention you're asking to receive.

Technique 11: Treat Yourself

One reason those with low self-esteem have difficulty in relationships is that they are waiting for their partner to feel special. While it's great to have someone give the recognition you deserve, it is crucial to feel also special. Don't wait to see if someone else will treat you. Make a plan for an entire day a week when you take time to pamper yourself. You could leave for your work fifteen minutes earlier so that you can indulge in a delicious coffee before heading to work, or take an indulgence in a bubble bath containing candlelight and oils to end a tiring day. Get yourself the dress or belt you've been looking at for many months. Self-love is about knowing that you're unique. You deserve to be loved, you just need to work for it.

Method 12: Learn to Understand Your Life Story

Since the time you were born and your surroundings began shaping your experiences. The people you met in your early childhood as well as the experiences you encountered and the way you developed were a part of your current self. Most people are struggling with their personal narrative. People may view their history with sadness or anger in particular if they've suffered a rough life.

When you begin to appreciate yourself, you should also take note of the things that have made your character into who you have become today. That doesn't mean you must be awed by the struggles you endured. It is helpful to put them in an overall perspective. Someone who suffered abuse in their youth may be grateful that they are stronger now in relationships and are able to can stand in their own defense. A person who was attacked by a dog may be able to explain the reason they're afraid of dogs.

Making your life story complete is like making a puzzle. Each experience you have were able to record within your subconscious even if you don't be conscious of it. When you reflect on your life, these fragments will eventually be put in place. Once you have a better understanding of your identity and the reasons you're this way, you will be able to be more grateful for yourself.

Chapter 11: Joy Self-Acknowledgment

Accepting Oneself

While it is a part of self-acknowledgement, it isn't the same thing as self-esteem. Although self-esteem refers to how important, or valuable, we consider ourselves, self-acknowledgement implies an affirmation of self as a person of truth. When we are confident in our self-esteem, we're able to take in all aspects of ourselves- - not just the positive, but also the and more "regard capable" components. Self-acknowledgement is certain, and an acknowledgment of all ability. We can recognize our flaws limitations, limitations, and weaknesses however, this awareness does doesn't interfere with our ability to accept our self-awareness completely.

I often inform my clients that if they really want to boost their self-esteem, they need to examine the parts of themselves they're not yet willing to acknowledge. In the end the process of loving ourselves more (or doing better expressions with yourself) is mostly it to do with self-acceptance. When we stop judging ourselves that we will be able to verify that we are feeling confident about our own self-worth. That's that I believe self-esteem will increase naturally after we stop being so hard with ourselves? This is exactly why self-acknowledgement is certainly more than self-esteem, and I believe to be essential to our happiness and overall well-being.

What are the issues that determine our Self-Acceptance (or the lack of it) in the first place?

As children, we have self-esteem we're able to be acknowledged only in the sense that we feel affirmed by our parents. Studies have revealed that, before 8 years old we are unable to identify an unmistakable independent sense of self-esteem - which is distinct from the one it was handed from our parents. Therefore, if our folks were not able, or reluctant, to impart the understanding that we were very all right and adequate - independently, that is, of our difficult-to-control, in some cases errant practices - we were prepared to see ourselves as undecided. The respect we received from our family members could be an impact on the way we behaved, and sadly we found that the majority of our actions did not meet their expectations. So, having a clear understanding of these unacceptable behaviors, we began to think of ourselves as inadequate in many ways.

Additionally, unfriendly and affectionate assessments could, and now and then get beyond simply expressing displeasure with bad behavior. For instance, guardians can give us the message that we're selfish or aren't beautiful enough, smart enough, and "pleasant" sufficient . . . Etc. Due to what the majority of psychological experts agree is an unpretentious kind of psychological maltreatment, we are all conditioned to see ourselves as merely worthy. This is why we learn to view various parts of ourselves negatively and hide the stinging the feelings of disapproval that are a result of our guardians who are too critical. Self-criticism is the root of the greater part of the issues we, as adults, we create for ourselves.

Considering how the human mind functions is almost impossible not to raise ourselves according in the same way as we were at the beginning. If our guardians treated us in a way that was harmful to us and we became adults we will discover many ways to endure that unrelenting admonition towards us. If a lot of the time we are judged, disregarded and chastised, accused or physically punished, we'll in one way or other devise a way to deal with our self-deflection. Therefore whenever (metaphorically or otherwise) you "beat ourselves to death," we are regularly following our parents who are leading the way. Dependent on them a lot as we grew older and thus undergoing minor influences that could challenge their different views of us, we felt generally obliged to accept their negative views as significant. It's not to say that they never made us feel bad. The guardians of the past were known to be a bit snarky whenever we do something that is troubling them rather than be able to recognize us for our more positively-oriented, well-organized social habits. When we are analyzing our current perceptions of our own self, we also need to consider the discontent and criticism we might have received from family members and other family members, teachers and, in particular our peers whom (battling to answer their own questions about themselves) would not hesitate to ridicule our weaknesses at any time we "uncovered" the flaws. In any event, it is reasonable to assume that most of us begin in a state of maturity with a certain negative outlook. We all have a tendency to blame ourselves or believe that we are in some way flawed. This is like saying that we all, in whatever size, share the negative consequences of the similar constant "infection" that is self-doubt.

Being able to accept ourselves with a sincere attitude (regardless of our shortcomings) could have been in our genes if our parents sent out a overwhelmingly convincing message about us. Plus we were raised in a typically positive atmosphere. This isn't the case, in fact it is our responsibility to learn the best ways we can "certify" ourselves to justify our essential ok-ness. Furthermore I'm not suggesting that we must only validate ourselves. It doesn't have nothing to do with facing the truth, just that we get over our inclination to always make an unpopular decision on our own self-worth. If we have ever encountered as our normal state of being, personal fulfillment and genuine feeling of peace We must first be able to meet the expectations of people who expect total self-acknowledgement that is not suited to us.

Self-acknowledgement and joy work in tandem

According to Robert Holden, notes in his book Happiness Now! "Joy and self-acknowledgement are interdependent. In reality, your level of self-acknowledgement will determine your level of happiness. The more self-acknowledgement you show the greater satisfaction you'll be able to acknowledge, acknowledge and cherish. In turn, you will experience the same amount of joy that you recognize that you are deserving of it."

More than anything else, gaining self-awareness is a prerequisite for developing self-sympathy. When we are able to recognize and excuse ourselves from things we thought to be our fault, will be able to build our relationship with self, which up to now was a mystery.

To take on a more loving self-esteem which is the most important sign of self-acknowledgement - we must realize that up to now, we've believed that we were required to demonstrate our worth to others similar to the way we initially believed that we were required to be a submissive experts that was our guardians. Our acceptance of certain actions from then on (misinformed and/or not) is a reflection of the history of our family's restrictive affection for each other.

An exercise like the real-life investigation of what I call our near "widespread situation" certainly increases self-sympathy. It's simple sympathy that can use to be more loving of ourselves, and see ourselves as worthy of praise and respect by the "righteousness" in our willingness to confront (and fight against) the things we've made difficult to accept in relation to ourselves.

It is possible to say that we all have "conditional affection scars" that date back to a long time ago. We're all in the roles of the "walking wounded." Furthermore, this acknowledgement of humankind's normality will help to inspire us in specific feelings of recurrent generosity and altruism directed towards not just ourselves but to those around us too.

In the direction of a more self-accepting way of life, we must start by telling ourselves (frequently and, best of all - with ever-growing confidence) that, despite the overwhelming majority of our contradictory and one-sided self-referential belief systems, we have achieved the best that we can. In evaluating, we must look at any lingering notions of blame along with our numerous self-reflexes and insults. It is important to ask our own beliefs about what it is that we are not able to acknowledge in about ourselves and as the agents of our own recuperation we should bring compassion and understanding for every self-dismissal , or refusal. Therefore, we should begin to eliminate false feelings of shame and blame based on gauges that did not accurately reflect what could reasonably be expected from us in the moment.

The well-known French expression, "Tout comprendre, c'est all excuses" (precisely, "to comprehend everything is to be excused from every one") can be described as a rule that we must use regardless of the situation, as much in our own lives as others. In this way we will be able to discover the reason why we were compelled to behave with a particular objective in mind. And in the end, we'll be able to pardon ourselves for our actions and refraining from repeating it later.

Self-acceptance is a process that demands that we begin to realize the fact that we're not at blame anyone for particular thing, regardless of whether the case is that it's our words or knowledge or ever-changing practices. Our actions have been stymied by a mix of science and foundation. In the pursuit of progress, we have the ability to and in most cases consider take responsibility for the ways we've harmed or hurt other people. In any event, if we want to strive toward self-acceptance and effectively, we must do it by embracing compassion and pardoning our hearts. It is important to comprehend the specifics of our inner programming up at that moment that we couldn't have behaved differently.

"Self-Pardon"

To be free and to achieve a state of infinite self-acknowledgement, it is essential to recognize the mental state that is one of "self-pardon" to our sins (regardless of whether they are true or not). Then, we can realize that there is no reason to be pardoned. We were not able to ignore what we could have thought we knew prior to that, we were, we could say, forever free of guilt - doing our best possible in the context of (1) the nature of what was inborn (or hard-wired) within our minds, (2) how convincing our desires (and feelings) had been at the moment in addition to (3) what we believed we were able to accept about ourselves.

The thing that, in the end is the one that determines the most risky behavior is a result of regular mental protections. Furthermore, it isn't remorseful for us to hold ourselves accountable or even and hold ourselves in shame for the manner of conduct that we were believed we were required to protect ourselves from disgrace, anxiety or even exuberant pain.

Yet, it is an essential part of our nature and needs to be effectively coordinated if we want to be fully. So long as we do not admit - or even obligate to recognize the split-off of parts of ourselves the self-acknowledgement we have been conditioned to accept will be elusive.

If we're able to think about the genesis of these dull, passive parts in our bodies, any self-reflection to them becomes painful and humiliating as well. In reality, for the most part, everyone has prohibited (and possibly, ridiculous) motives and goals regardless of whether they're harming someone we consider off-putting, exercising unbridled control over other people or (for certain!) repeatedly being naked on the boulevards. Once we're able to be aware of that we are all the while accepting our bodies without any conditions. Recognizing that no matter how unusual or unlucky, the vast majority of what we call "malicious imaginations" are probably just a few imaginings that make that allow for the occurrence of insults, damage or the hardships we've faced during the previous time, we are able to consider the "variations" as as being quite common.

Furthermore, even when we begin to recognize our darker aspect, we can retain control of how our personal parts are communicated to others - which is to say, in ways which will guarantee our wellbeing for ourselves and others. As long as we've been able to reconnect with our most authentic, deepest authentic self, we'll come from a place of love and concern. This means that it is not our responsibility to act in a way that would harm our inherent inclination to feel empathy and the resonant proof of humanity in general. Integrating and accepting our various aspects is a remarkable experience. Furthermore that we or, more accurately our self-images will never feel any longer separated from the rest of humanity, any reason to harm them disappears.

It is obvious that self-acknowledgement is not a reason to the self-improvement process in that way. It isn't tied to "fixing" any aspect of ourselves. Self-acknowledgement is simply affirming our own identity, with all the strengths and weaknesses we might have at the time.

The issue with a strong emphasis on personal growth is that this kind of focus will always make self-acknowledgement more restrictive. Furthermore, we can never feel safe or sufficiency if our self-esteem is contingent on constantly striving to improve ourselves. Self-acknowledgement is based on this moment in the present, not planned for the future like: "I'll be alright when . . ." or "When I have achieved . . . I'll be fine." Self-acknowledgement means that you are okay with no limitations that are not there. It's not to ignore or minimize our weaknesses or shortcomings however we perceive them as unimportant to our very existence.

In the end It's us- and only us - who set the standards to recognize ourselves. In addition, if we choose to stop reviewing ourselves or "keeping the track of" ourselves, we are able to adopt a mindset of non-evaluative pardoning. If we eschew the habit of studying and re-reading ourselves - trying to more to comprehend our past habits and behaviors in a way that is humane - we'll realize that there's no need to forgive (recall, "Tout comprendre ..."). In the end, we'll be able to make a promise to improve in the future but we must admit ourselves as we are now, paying not much attention to our shortcomings.

But I'm not able to prove enough to recognize and appreciate ourselves while still focusing on self-awareness throughout our lifetime. Being content with the way it is doesn't mean you're not able to change or make improvements that make us more feasible, or enhance our (and other people's) lives. Self-acknowledgement does not have to be connected to the modifications. We don't have to prove our self-acknowledgement in a timely manner simply modify how we perceive ourselves. Thus, changing our behavior can be viewed as solely the result of our individual preferences which isn't necessary for a more self-respecting self.

It's all about being from a completely different source. If self-acknowledgement is "earned," an outcome of our squeezing ourselves and putting ourselves in a position of being constantly at risk. The ongoing "work" of acceptance of ourselves will never be completed. even a grade of A+ in whatever task we're using to assess ourselves may provide us with an instant respite from our responsibilities. Because the message we're sending to ourselves that our contribution is only useful as the most recent achievement. It's impossible to "land" in a state of self-acknowledgement because we've defined our purpose for this recognition as eternal.

When we abide by such idealistic standards regardless it is possible that we are accepting how our loved ones treated us. But, we're not being ourselves or being a good person to ourselves and believed our family members were not able enough to be accommodating.

For the final part it is only when we're prepared to express our unconditional approval through a greater display of self-acceptance and focusing more on our strengths than negatives- are we able to finally forgive ourselves for our mistakes, as well as we let go of the need to be endorsed by others. We've certainly made mistakes. But , then, so has everybody else. Our individuality isn't like our mistake (for this kind of linkage could suggest an unfortunate case in the realm of "mistaken identities"!)

In the end, there's no reason why we shouldn't be able to make a decision now to alter the core perception of our identity. In addition, we might need to be reminded that our diverse flaws are our human nature. If each of our failings and imperfections were to disappear, my favorite idea is that we'd immediately disappear into the white light of the planet. This way, in seeking to be acknowledged for our true self perhaps we'll have to take pride in our weaknesses. In all likelihood, were we a victim of criticism at all we wouldn't have the opportunity to pass the level of this incredibly human level.

Living a conscious Life

If you continue to live a an active life, you'll be able to lead an actual life that is full of satisfaction and joy. Living a conscious life implies that you're evaluating your choices, exercises and decisions. You're making conscious choices based on your character and your own truth.

How do you define conscious?

An active life a deliberate and well-thought-out life. It's about listening to yourself, and then deciding on your next steps.

You're pondering the reason behind what you're doing, analyzing the reasons behind your actions. You're not floating in the midst of your life, but instead you're making a deliberate, deliberate move.

Imagine walking into a shop without knowing what you're likely to buy. Being conscious means thinking about an essential list of food items and understanding what you're going to cook for dinner this week. Being conscious is like buying tickets for a plane before you reach the plane terminal, knowing which plane you'll be taking and where you'll be going.

Surprisingly enough, the majority of people don't follow this line of thinking. They are governed by the rules of their families or follow the rules of society. the public to follow.

What are the benefits of living in a way that is purposeful?

Most of us don't have the opportunity to live our lives in a conscious manner. From the moment we are born to the day we die and we decide how to live our lives. The people around us push our lives to become a certain kind of person or to seek out certain food items and choose a certain career. We are told by society that success is derived by living within a specific community, attaining an expert level, buying a certain type of home or driving a particular automobile.

Beyond society and family, the organizations of the world are looking for our money so that they can offer us goods and fulfill investors' needs. If you live your life in a way that is intentional you are able to confront and question every aspect of your life. You'll be able to make the right choice and discard the things that aren't a match for you.

What do I think of awareness?

A way to discover the light is to be in complete darkness. I was in the dark for the majority throughout my entire life believing the fact that whatever my parents and friends allowed me to know was true.

I chose a job based on the salary.

I chose a romantic relationship based on conventions and culture.

I decided to pursue a job based on the level of respect it received.

I bought a home based on my society's guidance to behave as it did.

Then , all of these began to unravel then I started to consider whether each of the assertions I'd been told was valid. Perhaps no one really is aware of what's best for us? What been successful for one person and for one family or even an age group of people may not be suitable for another person?

Chapter 12: Self-Growth

Dreams and Hopes

Everyone has something wants to achieve in the near future or something you'd like to accomplish but taking that decision isn't easy. The first step is be convinced that you will succeed in everything you set your heart and soul into. There are some dreams that you've got however, you don't believe they're real. Perhaps you don't know you It is important to get to know yourself, and to know what the best can be made of you. Being yourself is about understanding your beliefs and knowing what you desire and feel about. Based on your personality and what you believe is important to you determine your goals and goals, and before putting in place the right plan to assist you in keeping your hopes alive and reach your goals. Being aware of what you're capable of and how you can utilize your capabilities to meet your goals boosts confidence in yourself and helps you to keep it because achieving your dreams will not happen in a single day. It requires a continuous setting of goals and then achieving them. The step-by-step process that is clearly laid out will make you feel more at ease and makes you feel more confident in your self.

A Vision Board

Vision boards are an image that showcases your achievements in your life and what they can do for you. Write your vision board, with a focus on the things you want to attain or be and be, but your primary goal should be on how your dreams bring you joy rather than the tangible things bring you. This is because self-esteem focuses on the inner feeling. however, your vision board should contain everything that drives you. Consider your goals in areas like relationships, education, career financial, travel and health, in addition to other things. You may decide to create one large vision board that covers each of these areas or you can have multiple boards that are specific to each of the areas. As your dreams don't end once you've completed writing your vision board, make sure you leave room for further.

Visualization

When you have created the vision board must not be stored in a secure location. It is advisable to have the space in your home you believe is sacred for display of your vision board. This will ensure that you are able to see the vision board daily and at least a few times per daily. Each time you glance at the board, you imagine what you wrote and then register it in your subconscious mind. It is repeated each when you come across it, which allows you to be more connected with the goals you've set. It also helps you be aware of what you've achieved and what you've not so that you can be sure of your commitment and accountability.

Setting Self Esteem Goals

You've got goals and you've got the plan to be able to achieve these goals. In order to increase your self-esteem, then it's important to establish goals for self-esteem. You have to take responsibility for your course you're on towards improvement in self-esteem. The goals you set must be specific and measurable. Consider something you value and that gives the meaning you seek in your life. Take, for example, the relationship between your parents. Look at how that relationship is impacting your life negatively and how it affects how you feel. Imagine what you would like the relationship to look as, and then set objectives that will tell you precisely what you want or need to improve in your relationship and how the relationship affect you. Be aware that improving your self-esteem is the main goal However, there are it is important to set self-esteem goals that will ensure you're doing your best to achieve the ultimate aim. For example, if you're heading to town there are towns must be passed through before reaching the exact location. By passing through the tiny town in the process assures you that you're headed towards your ultimate destination. This is why it is crucial to establish self-esteem goals.

Smart Target

Human beings want to be the best results, and this is achieved by setting goals and reaching them. Every day, we set targets regarding how to handle relationships, the use of time, purchasing a house as well as getting the job done. Each of these areas requires focus, so it is crucial to set the right priorities and sets goals. The targets set must be able to manage the events that occur in the course of one's daily life. The event is not due to chance and coincidence. So, the goals set must be well-thought out in the sense that they are not based on coincidences and possibilities. They should also have aligned with the ideals that the individual who is executing them. So, those who support you should be included or considered. There is no need to create goals that cannot be accomplished because the person who is responsible for the execution is not comfortable.

Create Smart Target

The goals you're setting must be based on a goal that is sensible. The objectives must be stated in a manner that you are aware of the goals you must achieve. In the case above the moment you get to town X you will know that you've made an important step towards your goal You must get to the town so that you can consider yourself as working towards achieving the destination. Your goals must be quantifiable and you must be aware of when you've reached or not. If you're being considered to be trusted by your partner as your self-esteem goals is met, then you must be confident that your partner is trusting your actions. For instance, he trusts you when you inform your partner that you're late because you had to visit an acquaintance. The objectives should be achievable and is not a goal that takes a long time to reach. It shouldn't be a desire to consume all your energy and time as it is impossible to accomplish the goals. Also, the goals should be achievable and realistic so they are achievable You must be aware of your own capabilities so that you are aware of the things you can do and what you can't. When you set the objectives, make sure you are aware of them. The deadline for achieving the goal must be accomplished should be defined to ensure that you are working within a certain timeframe.

Short-Term and Long-Term Goals

When setting goals when setting goals, it is crucial to set both long-term and short-term goals since they impact the individual's progress and growth. Long-term targets last over a longer period of time and act as a motivation to improve yourself such as having a house that is a long-term objective, your mind on the right track to utilize your earnings effectively to ensure that you are saving each month to meet the goal. If you keep saving and save, you will feel like you have control over the future, and this gives you a sense of satisfaction about it. Therefore, it is essential to have at least one long-term objective you want to attain. These goals can also help you to establish a an overall direction you want to achieve.

Long term goals cannot be achieved by themselves since they are generally vague and abstract. They are usually achieved over a long period of time so when they are not compared with short term goals and if they're not checked, they'll only be achieved in part. Short-term targets must be set so that they are in line with the long-term goals. For example, you could set the goal of building a home in five years. After formulating the cost, the house is achievable by making a deposit of at least $500 into your account each month. The short-term goal can be defined as a monthly deposit of $500 to your account each month. So, it is important to combine short-term and long-term goals to achieve better results.

30 Day Self-Esteem Challenge

Sometimes, you feel like you are not worth it which can impact your ability to go on everyday routine. It's sometimes beneficial to participate in activities that increase self-esteem, so that we can return to normal and engage in normal ways with our loved ones and friends as well as achieve our goals at work and keep working to construct an enormous house for the family. These things can't be accomplished by someone who is not confident of oneself. So, boost your self-esteem by completing a self-esteem exercise more often.

30-Day Challenge

* Look at yourself and evaluate the things that make you feel not feel comfortable about your self. If it's a sensation or an experience Try to give the feeling a name that accurately describes it.

• Ask yourself what about the situation or thing that is making you feel uncomfortable affects your feelings.

• Consider what you could do to change the circumstances.

Note down the elements or areas of your daily life that are affected by your circumstances.

Pick a pen and create a vision board that outlines how you could change the circumstances

* On your vision board, list the items that give you confidence in yourself , and not just provide you with material satisfaction.

Conclusion

Your fate is in your control. It's up to you to control your life, your feelings and the circumstances that you are faced with and navigate your way across the finish line.

There's no reason to rethink your decision or be afraid to take this risk in the event that you fail. It's inevitable to fail regardless of whether you want it to or not, but it should not be something is used to determine who you are or decide whether or not you want to take chances for the next time. Failure is a learning experience, you must learn what failures provide, analyze the data and consider the ways you could have handled differently. You can be sure that next time will have the success you seek.

Everyone is unique, and comes with their own individual traits and imperfections. Find yourself and love what you're made of and appreciate what you have to give for the rest of humanity. Your talents are already there, you just have to make the effort to discover them without letting any negative or weak aspects to hinder your progress. As human beings, we tend to put too focus on the negative, but too little on positive aspects. Don't let your shortcomings obscure your potential. What a dull and depressing the world would look if everyone was created the same way and had the same talents and talents, and perfectly in every aspect. Everyone has something unique to contribute and that's what makes us so diverse and fascinating species. The key to all this is to recognize your own strengths and recognize your weaknesses and work hard to develop those skills.

If you're someone with a negative self-image, don't just sit in a corner, get involved and start doing something now that you can be proud of yourself in the future. You are the only one who decides how you perceive yourself, and you are the only one who can make changes to the things you're not happy about. Recognize the issue and act to change this problem. The sooner you take action then, the quicker you'll grow into the amazing charismatic, confident, confident person that you were created on Earth to become.

You are the only person you have in every aspect. Do not allow anyone to make you feel inadequate Stand up for yourself and tell them that you're exceptional and deserve to be treated with respect. What other people think of you is not their concern but theirs. Make yourself satisfied and believe that something is true and be a part of it Make decisions, and never give up even when you fail and walk your head up. You weren't created to be a part of the background You were given a voice . So make the most of it and share your opinion, even though you might appear silly in the end.

Get a balanced diet and exercise routine. Your body and mind require to release stress. The nutrients and oxygen will give you enough power and energy and stamina to tackle whatever life throws at you. A healthy mind and body helps you concentrate on the things that matter to achieve those goals.

Don't be a comparison to other people. You are a unique individual and you have to recognize that. Watch how more confident individuals handle certain situations , and then learn from their experiences. Don't be a victim of criticism, but don't let the criticisms to heart. Take them in, process them, and take what you can from them and then go on.

Do not compromise your beliefs or believe in the name of being accepted. We are not created to blend in, but to stand out, and you ought to.

Confidence begins in your own mind. It is essential to be content and content with yourself, and recognize your own capabilities before you can expect anyone else to. Be proactive and change your behavior and be content with your self first, and confidence will be there. Bring positive thoughts to your mind and imagine positive things happening for yourself and you'll see them coming to you. Do not expect anything less than what you desire. Expectation is a powerful force that you must make use of for your benefit.

Of course, there will be moments when you feel like you're unraveling but these are small challenges that you face in the path to the success you've been seeking. Keep your mind and body positive. Even when you are feeling blue wear your confident strut and keep your head up high. You will notice that your mind will follow in your footsteps .Your mind will do whatever you tell do and when you direct it in the right direction, you will be able to experience what it is like to truly live.

Confidence gives you to interact with new people, engage in conversations with strangers, and you never have a clue about what's coming up. It is common for us to get caught in the mud in our personal relationships, and shut our friends out. Invite them into your life and show the side of you that they've never seen before and spark that fire. Let loose a bit, be welcoming and open to welcoming new people to your life. They might not stay for long, but they might end up staying for the rest of your life.

Be ready for every chance you can get and grasp it with both hands, and even failing, but at least you won't be left with regrets over what could be. Make sure you are confident in your choices even if the decision doesn't pan out for you, so take it as it is, but do it again. Don't put off your goals in waiting to find the ideal moment. we all know that the moment is never perfect , and there always will be some sort of hurdle. If you can realize you're using this method to avoid the fear of failure and the fear of failure and failing, the better. Take the plunge and embrace your fears. the leap. You will be amazed by how happy you feel.

I really hope that this book has helped those lacking self-esteem and confidence to understand that they're in control of their lives and that the earlier they feel confident in their self-esteem and believe that they're capable of accomplishing great things, the more quickly their lives will really begin. Everyone is equal to everyone or anyone else. Some people have only just discovered what their strengths are and have embraced their strengths to the fullest but it's not enough for those who are yet to recognize this, and put aside the thoughts of " what is if" as well as "if you only" and just shut your eyes and leap. Let the world see your brilliance in all its splendor. We all have brilliance in various ways. And what you consider insignificant might be something that many people only imagine having.

You are the keeper of your life and master. You are in charge of your body, mind , and your emotions. You are the one who decides your destiny and how others perceive you. Get up and take an oath The world is waiting for you.